Giving Away My Joy

THE PSALMIST MODEL OF SPIRITUAL JOY
A COMMENTARY ON PASTORAL LEADERSHIP

Dr. Wilma Robena Johnson

Foreword by
Dr. Charles G. Adams
and
Afterword by
Dr. Riggins R. Earl, Jr.

Joy To You!

Wilma JJ

Orman Press
Lithonia, Georgia

Giving Away My Joy

The Psalmist Model of Spiritual Joy
A Commentary on Pastoral Leadership

by
Dr. Wilma Robena Johnson

Copyright © 2005
Dr. Wilma Robena Johnson

ISBN: 1-891773-60-7

Scripture quotations are taken from THE HOLY BIBLE, *New Revised Standard Version,* or are the author's paraphrase of that version unless noted otherwise.

Printed in the United States of America

10 9 8 7 6 5 4 3 2 1

Publishing Services Provided By
Orman Press, Inc.
Lithonia, Georgia

Acknowledgements

To God be the glory for all blessings!

To my husband, David L. Johnson, and my sons, Davey and Brian, who love me still, I am so grateful. For the inspiration from my mom and all my family members who prayed for me, those living and those who have completed this earthly journey—thank you.

Special thanks to Marsha Hathaway, Sylvia Rose and the Ecumenical Theological Seminary staff for their partnership in completing this project. Special thanks to Dorothy Ward, Remonia Chapman, Dr. Tony Henderson, Dr. Ronald Bobo, Dr. Warren Stewart and Dr. Jeremiah Wright, who constantly encouraged me to get this work done. Special thanks to my editor, Cheryl Edwards and the staff at Orman Press.

Words are inadequate to describe the help provided by Dr. Charles G. Adams, Dr. Riggins Earl and my dissertation team—Dr. Ken Harris, Dr. Forest Harris and Dr. David Swink. Thank you so very much!

Much love, joy and gratitude to the congregation of New Prospect Missionary Baptist Church in Detroit, Michigan for your participation in the ministry of joy that God has given me. Thanks to all ministers, my staff, the leadership and the entire membership for your powerful prayers and encouraging the continued education of your pastor. Thanks for supporting my time away from pastoral duties for seminary courses, research and writing.

I am grateful for the prayers of my prayer partner, Rev. DeeDee Coleman, family, friends, other pastors and church members during the five-year process of completing the requirements for the Doctor of Ministry degree and writing this book.

If there is someone I forgot to mention, please accept my joy. To all who read this book, may joy bells keep ringing in your soul.

Rev. Wilma R. Johnson

Table of Contents

Foreword

Having known the Rev. Dr. Wilma R. Johnson for a number of years as a colleague in ministry, I can say without fear of contradiction that her life and work are a profound blessing to humankind because of the generosity and contagion of her charismatic spirit of love, truth and joy. She presents in these cogently written pages the story and analysis of her pastoral symphony and synergy of heart, head, sermon, song, service, love, joy and peace.

She is a faithful servant of God in this present age, which tempts us away from love and joy by the futile substitutions of mechanical communications, digital entertainments and depersonalized distractions. Her pastoral achievements have been generated by the wise, post-modern re-visions of conventional, modern evasions of human affection, warm friendship and personal involvement in the lives and fortunes of those human beings whom one should seek to know by face, by name and by their unique situation.

Pastors today see their mega congregations as a nameless and faceless mass; but Dr. Johnson sees them, knows them, loves them and serves them as persons, human beings who reincarnate the incarnation of Jesus Christ. She loves the masses of her church as if they were an individual, and she loves and serves the individual as if she or he were the whole universe. Such is the intensity, sensitivity and sincerity of her powerful presence in and beyond her anointed pulpit.

It is said that all literature is, in essence, biography. Certainly, this worthy literature that represents a beneficial "case study" for teaching the techniques of effective church ministry, is simultaneously the biography of a strong, achieving, preaching pastor who has transposed personal biography into pastoral theology, methodology and doxology. Is there any wonder that those who read these pages will not only be enlightened and instructed, but also deeply stirred and strangely warmed and moved to love, praise and thank God for the marvelous author, candid auto-biographer, gifted raconteur, loving spirit and spectacular pastor that Dr. Johnson is? As you read these pages, do not conform them to the narrow mold of your own limited understanding, but enter her larger universe of faith that clings to Christ. It is a place where hope is confident that the "best is yet to be" and love makes all humankind one family in God with liberty, equality and opportunity for all!

What a blessing is this book, not only to preachers and pastors, but more importantly to all persons who desire to help make and keep human life more human and more holy!

Charles G. Adams, Pastor
Hartford Memorial Baptist Church
Detroit, Michigan

Preface

Spiritual joy plays a significant role in the leadership vision I bring to the pastorate of New Prospect Missionary Baptist Church of Detroit. I embrace the spirituality and theology of the Hebrew psalmist as an authentic model of pastoral leadership based on the relational qualities of spiritual joy. I have adopted a model of pastoral leadership in acts of ministry described as the *Psalmist Model of Spiritual Joy*. God has shown me that one can positively affect church growth, worship attendance and ministry participation through the psalmist leadership style because people will receive and respond to an intangible—the giving away of joy.

In applying this model, the relational and reciprocal qualities of spiritual joy shape expressions of worship, stewardship, counseling, and social outreach in ministry. As I envision and live out my pastoral function, a communal sharing of joy occurs between the congregation and me as we give and receive joy from encounters with God and each other in the course of our spiritual journey. I see my role as "giving away my joy" to encourage others to share their spiritual joy in worship, ministry and Christian service. As pastor, my goal is to create a congregation of members who constantly give away their joy to draw people to Christ.

The transformative experience of joy is a repetitive theme through most of the Hebrew Psalms. Theological commentaries on the Psalms confirm that spiritual joy radically alters one's spiritual perspective and social existence. What follows within the pages of this book is my reflection on the experiences of joy in my spiritual life, and how these experiences interrelate to the style of pastoral leadership I have adopted at New Prospect Missionary Baptist Church.

When I began serving as the senior pastor of the New Prospect Missionary Baptist Church, the membership roster listed one thousand members. In five years, the membership tripled. Every Sunday at 7:30 a.m. and 11:00 a.m., I would teach, preach, pray and sing. Record crowds have filled the sanctuary every Sunday since March 8, 1999. As the new pastor, I examined my surroundings and met with church leaders and members to understand how we might sustain the spiritual growth of New Prospect Missionary Baptist Church. My chief concern was to understand how my pastoral style of leadership affected church growth.

I learned that several factors contributed to our growth: the demographics of the community, New Prospect's continuous presence in the community, the effectiveness of leadership and our strong ministry outreach. After reflecting upon these growth factors, I realized that a pastoral leadership style is the most crucial to congregational growth.

I have often looked over the congregation and asked myself: "Why do they keep packing this place Sunday after Sunday? What are the reasons for this church growth?" Fellow pastors have even asked me to share what I was doing at the church. "How do you do it?" they asked. *Giving Away My Joy: The Psalmist Model of Spiritual Joy* is my answer.

I will share the significant role pastoral leadership style plays in church growth, particularly in light of my vision of "giving away my joy." I will describe my personal spiritual journey, and the characteristics and context of New Prospect Missionary Baptist Church, where my pastoral style has been most effective for over five years. I will lead you in taking a close look at Jesus' leadership style and define what it means to be a good steward of spiritual joy. I will then introduce the Psalmist Model of Spiritual Joy and share the joy of my pastoral journey at New Prospect. I have included a review of pastoral leadership literature and feedback from hundreds of my members as evidence that joy works. In closing, I will share my personal reflections. I have listened and heard. It is a delight to share what I have learned. In the appendix are examples of tools that will help you implement this model in your church and statistical results from surveys conducted with my congregation.

My prayer is that you will discover the power of the psalmist model and join me in giving away joy. There are many people whose lives are joyless. Through the Psalmist Model of Spiritual Joy, you can fill their empty, aching hearts with God's love, and then grow them into spiritually mature and loving servants of Christ.

Chapter One

My Spiritual Journey

Upon reviewing my spiritual journey, I can identify several aspects of my life that shaped my leadership style. I describe my style as the Psalmist Model of Spiritual Joy. It has been created and molded by everything I have experienced. I am a pastor with faith, joy, a testimony, a song and a story. Yet, I know that the Lord is still preparing me for the next phase of my life. I would like to share my personal journey, where even as a child some of the qualities I possess as a pastor were present.

I was born prematurely, December 23, 1951, under a bridge in Millville, New Jersey. My parents were teenagers. I am the oldest of six girls, and I had the unfortunate responsibility of taking care of my sisters. It was a joyless burden. The very notion of having children of my own never entered my mind for years. I had to baby-sit, feed and stay home from school just to take care of my sisters. I could change a diaper in record time; baby on my lap, powder and Vaseline nearby and pins in my mouth.

Joy in Singing

I was raised Methodist in a little town called Port Norris, New Jersey. We faithfully attended John Wesley Methodist Church. I participated in Sunday school, Vacation Bible School, and I sang in the choir. My mother played the piano for her group, "The Jubileers." How I wanted to sing with them! I imagined singing and traveling from church to church with them. I remember entering talent shows and oratorical competitions either singing or reciting poetry. I remember having to memorize the longest poems and speeches, especially for Youth Day, Christmas and Easter. Even then, I enjoyed speaking in front of people.

Port Norris was known for its oyster industry. It sat right on the Maurice River. There were always floods when the river overflowed. My church was located at the entrance of a section of rows of houses called, *Shellpile*. The people would shuck oysters and leave piles of shells. I remember the smell and watching other children play on them like piles of dirt.

Every Sunday we visited my Aunt Rosie and Grandma Delilah for dinner because they lived and worked in Shellpile. When my parents fought, my mother would always pack us up and go stay with one of them. While there, I had to prime the pump to get water. I had to take a jar and some change to buy kerosene for heat. Little bugs called "chinches" would bite me all night long. There was no joy and no sleep. I had to carry the red and white pot out to the outhouse in the morning because there were no bathrooms. After a few days, we would go back home.

My immediate family was fortunate to be one of the black families in Port Norris to have a house with a furnace and a bathroom. No doubt some even admired that green house on a hill, on the outskirts of Port Norris. I know some envied that well-kept green house owned by black folks. I was the one who kept the grass cut. I was the one who kept the hound dogs tied up. I was the one who made sure the hogs were fed and didn't get out. I was also the one who played "Red Light" with the kids and caught lightning bugs in mason jars. Because I was able to portray a life of balance, it looked real good from the outside. But on the inside, especially at night, there was no joy.

I enjoyed going to school. I missed being in school when I couldn't go. In the seventh grade, I represented my school in the National Spelling Bee competition in Philadelphia, Pennsylvania. I delivered the eighth grade graduation speech wearing a green beret and a pretty white dress. One of my teachers rewarded some of the excellent students by taking them to New York City to see the movie, "The Sound of Music." I was proud to be among them.

Why I Value Joy

As a young child, I longed for love and some joy. I lived in an abusive, alcoholic environment. My mother was very young when she became a wife and a mother. My father was young and illiterate. He was also very jealous, especially when he compared himself to his brothers and other men. If he thought a man was looking at my mother, she was accused of having an affair. He always looked for ways to show and prove to the world that he was the greatest. Unfortunately, he used liquor, his fists and negative words to promote himself. My father worked every day, no doubt looking forward to the weekend. Still, he always kept his day job working at the plant for J. M. Sand, and he eventually retired when his health began to fail after almost thirty years.

My dad also owned an establishment in Shellpile nicknamed "The Hole." It was a place where you could spend your money to dance and drink the night away. Every weekend my sisters and I would have to clean up The Hole. I hated the smell of smoke and liquor, but I'll never forget the music. I sure did enjoy the music playing on the jukebox while we worked. Songs like, "With Every Beat of My Heart" and "On The Outside Looking In" filled the air. I would sweep, sing and dream about performing on stage. As long as the music played, I could endure the sights and smells.

I dreaded Friday and Saturday nights because I knew what was going to happen when the car came in the driveway early in the morning. My dad would drink liquor, and then come home and beat, choke and fight with my mother. It seemed like every weekend to me. I knew he had a gun. I was afraid of him and his words, but that did not stop me from jumping on him and yelling to stop him from hurting our mother. Finally, after years of abuse, while a junior in high school, my mother packed us all up and we moved, physically leaving my dad behind.

I must say that as the years passed, I could not ignore the fact that I still loved and admired my dad. We spent years enjoying a healed relationship. He died November 2000, and I was with him when he drew his last breath. The Holy Spirit would not let me leave the hospital, and I am so glad for being obedient once again. I miss him and I think about him every day. I thank God that my dad witnessed my installation service as pastor of New Prospect. He told me the celebration was the biggest event he had ever attended. I know that his parents, Grandma Beanie and Grandpa Oney, smiled down on our brand new relationship.

I truly believe that the events connected with the abusive environment that I grew up in were all opportunities for growth. Only because of God's grace have I been able to survive those experiences and see how they increased my ability to care, love, comfort, forgive and relate to those whom I serve today. Because of those events, I also know that having joy in your life is priceless.

Learning to Care for Others

I watched my mother during those times. She was (and still is) determined that she would not be destroyed mentally, emotionally or physically. God blessed me to get over blaming her for my childhood. When my sisters were ill, I had to stay home from school to take care of them. When my dad didn't trust my mom to stay home, or they had a "love" moment (it appeared to me that they were always making babies), my dad would take her out with him. But when they returned, the usual battles continued. You could hear them in the driveway and on the back porch. When my parents fought, I would comfort my sisters by hugging them and covering their ears. I was trying to give them something. We would all cry together and hope it would soon stop. I remember having a baby in my arms, one holding on to my leg for dear life, and another calling me "Mama." I babysat my life away.

I hated living in Port Norris, New Jersey. I always knew that one day I would have joy in my life like what I saw in TV programs and read about in books. Thank God I could read. I loved to read. When there was a moment of peace and my sisters were sleeping, I would cook, wash, clean and read. I still have a book about animals that I was punished for ordering. The pictures brought some color and joy into my life. Although I did not fully understand all the circumstances then, I now know that my younger sisters needed me to love and care for them, and I was there.

Not Knowing How to Care for Myself

After graduating from high school, I attended college. I was hungry for love and started looking for it in all the wrong places and with all the wrong people. I exhausted myself trying to make myself whole and complete, yet I always walked away empty. I remember even taking the attention offered by my gynecologist as a sign of love. I kept thinking that if I kept changing men, I would be content. I remember the names of all of them. I even remember the locations that

I permitted myself to be taken to if I couldn't get there on my own. I also remember what I allowed them to do to me emotionally and physically. I kept telling myself that if I changed my preference of alcohol it would be better. I liked Singapore slings, but I found myself always going back to rum and coke. Surely, sooner or later I would find what I was looking for. I only discovered that the more I gave, the more they took, and the more I hurt.

I only attended college for two years because I went to too many parties and studied very little. When I finally let a man talk me into having sex for the first time, I got pregnant. I went to New York and got an abortion because it was illegal in New Jersey. The chaplain on campus assisted me with all the details. The entire situation was unbelievable. I tried to commit suicide. I remember the doctors, the hospital and the detectives. I finally dropped out of college.

I got a job in the insurance industry and worked my way up from Insurance Rater to Underwriter Assistant to Systems Analyst Specialist. But few knew that I still felt empty, joyless and dissatisfied.

My first bottle of liquor was called Cold Duck, and it was placed in my hands by a preacher. My first date rape was by a preacher. Being young and naïve, I almost started to believe that this behavior was the norm for ministers, or that maybe it would give me self-worth. Of course it did not. Deep within my spirit, somewhere in my mind, I knew this should not be happening to me.

I kept crying out for this self-violence to stop. I carried the mental and physical pain with me everywhere. When would it stop? I kept trying to find safety and security in other relationships. Year after year, I found myself on a rollercoaster ride, and I couldn't get off. I lacked the power and the will. I wandered through life joyless and empty without any direction. Why was I allowing others to call the shots in my life other than the Lord? My life was completely absorbed in being abused physically, emotionally and spiritually. One of the men in my life was a minister, and I did not know what to do.

I should hate preachers and all men of the cloth. Instead, God decided to make me a preacher so that others could witness and be comforted in the future by what God can do with a messed up child of God. I finally heard and listened to the voice of the Lord. I obeyed and put my life in God's wonderful hands.

Joy Is Possible

I remember an opportunity for spiritual growth that took place while I was in school. A classmate invited me to attend his church. I was raised in a Methodist church so this was the first time I attended a Baptist church. There was something in the air that attracted me. It was truly a joyous experience. The music, the preaching, the clapping and shouting all stirred something inside of me. I laughed and cried all at the same time. I finally felt alive, and I thought just maybe I could feel completely whole. I had never felt this way before.

That Sunday the pastor preached about "The Tongue" and I joined. I was later baptized by immersion and a new freedom in worshipping and praising the Lord entered my life.

At the age of twenty-one, I received the call into the ministry. I answered that command, and it has been the greatest decision I ever made in my entire life. My motto is "Jesus is the best thing that ever happened to me!" Mercy looked at me and saw beauty, potential and something that God could use. That day, I really felt loved. I finally realized the foundation of my strength, and this is what I try to communicate to others. I know who I am. I know I am God's daughter, and I am available to be used by the Source of my strength. I know today that Jesus is truly the center of my joy. I want to make a difference in this world. Maybe in some small way, I can have a positive influence on others. It is my daily prayer that they will find the joy that is missing from their lives.

I did not know that my grandmother had already declared that I would be a preacher when I was three years old. My favorite aunt, Aunt Lossie, revealed this information to me when I was thirty years old. What an affirmation! My grandmother, Grandma Robena, who we lovingly called Grandma Beanie, after whom I am named, looked at me and declared that one day I would be a preacher. I remember the first song she taught me to sing. It was the hymn, "How Great Thou Art." I had to stand up on a box in the church so they could see me, and sing my song. Knowing my grandmother said those blessed words confirmed once again that my feet were on solid ground. The Lord had indeed called me and there was no turning back.

Another life-shaping event that was an opportunity for spiritual growth was my first marriage. I learned patience and found power that I did not know I possessed. My first husband, who is deceased, was a substance abuser. It was the beginning of another nightmare. I remember walking into the bathroom and seeing a needle in his hand. Surely, this meant that I didn't do enough, love enough or give enough. So that is what I tried to do. For one second, I even thought that if I enjoyed cocaine with him, he would not inflict all those tears and sleepless nights upon me. What was wrong with me? Why couldn't I get him to stop putting that needle in his arm? I even went to church more and sang more. I prayed and read my Bible more because I thought that I must have failed at being a good wife. I was a Christian. I had already received the call into ministry, but if my husband loved cocaine more than me, it must be my fault.

I lost weight. I was ill all the time. I remember being in the hospital diagnosed with phlebitis. While lying there letting the doctors thin out my blood, the Lord came to me and said, "Why are you letting them do this to you? You know what you have to do." I checked myself out of the hospital. I knew I had done all I could do to save my marriage. Without putting the cocaine in my veins, I was addicted to the hurt and pain. The Lord rescued me once again. I survived three years of hell because within me was some joy waiting to surface.

If I have any success today as a minister it is because of these experiences. I have had some challenges. I have lived a life full of fear and failure. I have found myself in some very complicated circumstances. I never knew if my husband owed anyone money. I didn't know if they were watching our apartment. Anger would overtake me at times, and I would take the cocaine out of his wallet and briefcase and flush it down the toilet. At the time I didn't care and never thought about the horrific results or the position I was placing myself in. My mother and grandmother were terrified for my life. Most of the time, he was so high he didn't know what had happened to his supply.

We continued living in the same apartment for four months after I decided to leave him. When he did come home, we slept in the same bed, but words and action between us ceased. At night, I would turn my back to the door and trust in God. In spite of it all, I was able to stand tall in my weakness because the Lord gave me strength. When you think you have reached the end of the road, God always makes a highway out of difficult situations.

I Now Know Joy

One day in February 1983, the Lord gave David Johnson to me. The Lord continued loving me through Dave and has blessed us for twenty years. I fell in love with Jesus all over again and every time I look at Dave now, I'm in love. He is the most loving, compassionate and supportive person in my life. I am able to be all God wants me to be because of him.

Dave only wants to love me and bring joy to my life. He is very much aware and tells others that the Lord used him to get me to Detroit. He makes sure I am taken care of so the Lord can use me. I often ask myself, "What have I done to deserve someone like Dave?" I realize now, more than ever before, that I did absolutely nothing. The Lord is gracious, loving and kind despite my faults and shortcomings. God knew exactly what I needed for this journey. The Lord wanted me whole and full of joy so I could serve Him with my whole heart.

David Johnson and my first cousin, Michael were best friends. I always knew about Dave, but we had never met. I would always ask Michael how his friend Dave was doing. So one day Michael finally got us together. We dated six months, and I abruptly ended our relationship. I was afraid of the unknown. The relationship was going too great. It was wonderful, peaceful and unbelievable. I knew this wouldn't last so I did what I thought was right. I ended our relationship. I believed it was the right thing, but I was miserable. When the Lord brought me to my knees, and I realized that He was creating something I had no control over, I tried to talk to Dave, but he would not respond. So I prayed and waited patiently as I kept trying to reach him. Finally, he answered the phone three months later. Dave took me back and the Lord prepared us to do ministry together.

Dave's job moved him to Kansas City, Missouri. I followed him there, and we got married. Our first son was born in Kansas City. I worked and did ministry at the First Baptist

Church in Kansas City, under the late Dr. E. A. Freeman. Little did I know that the Lord was just laying the foundation for our entrance into Detroit, Michigan in 1989. God is so amazing! I am able to give exactly what the Lord desires of me because of the love and support I receive every single day from my husband and our two sons.

After twenty-two years of being out of school, I decided to go back. I felt God calling me to get my bachelor's and master's degrees. While in school, being a wife and mother of two young sons, I also served the Lord by working in ministry full time at the Hartford Memorial Baptist Church in Detroit, Michigan, under the Reverend Dr. Charles G. Adams. Through it all, I kept right on nurturing my family. We have accomplished much together. I have now completed by Doctor of Ministry degree. I know that the Lord is on my side, and I know I have the loving support of my family.

The Need for a Joyful Ministry

The experience of full-time ministry at Hartford Memorial Baptist Church was a life changing experience. I will always remember my first visit to the church. I decided that no one went to church at 7:30 in the morning. To my surprise, when I arrived at 8:00 a.m., I had to sit in the last pew of the balcony. I decided then that this church was too huge for me, and there were just too many people. I vowed to never return and started worshipping at another church in Pontiac, Michigan that I really wanted to join. I made an appointment with the pastor and explained to him my desire, my background and my joy. He immediately informed me that he had no idea what to do with a woman preacher. Disappointed, but certainly not crushed, I knew the Lord would provide a place where I could serve. The Lord had always provided that in the past, and I knew God to be faithful. So I prayed and asked the Lord: "What should I do now?" The Lord told me, "Go back to Hartford. I sent you to Hartford." Once again I was obedient. I did exactly what the Lord told me to. After several months, I made an appointment with Pastor Adams who welcomed me and my family with open arms. My youngest son was only four months old, but I contributed to the ministry as much as I could whenever I was asked.

When the time came for me to return to work, I found a job as a computer analyst. The first week on the job, I only worked three days because a problem developed with my babysitter. I had to stay home on Thursday and Friday. On Thursday morning, the phone rang. It was Dr. Charles G. Adams calling because the Holy Spirit told him to put me on his staff full-time. I accepted and on September 1, 1990, I became Assistant to the Pastor in Christian Nurture. Some members and colleagues wanted to know why Dr. Adams would put a woman without ordination or a degree on his staff. He replied, "Because the Holy Spirit does not dwell only in the ordained or degreed."

Working full-time in the ministry was new for me. Working for a great scholar and theologian like Dr. Adams was frightening. It didn't take long for me to discover who this man was and what gifts and talents he possessed. It also didn't take long for me to realize that my task was to support him wholeheartedly and to hold his arms up in ministry. What a blessing to my soul our relationship turned out to be! And I still add joy to his life today.

As I moved about the church and got to know the membership, I heard many voices crying out in the wilderness. I saw so many struggles, and I was there as a spiritual guide. Through Christ, I brought joy and a new fire to the life of the church as I used my gifts of encouragement and empowerment. I was able to show others that through Christ, we can do all things. I spent most of my time ministering to the sick and shut-in members in the hospitals and their homes. Embracing them with prayer and encouraging them to trust in God brought joy to my life. When families are faced with the illness and death of loved ones, words of comfort mean so much. My personal presence showed that the church and its pastor cared.

I thank God for every storm and every mountain in my life. I am thankful for all the fires and floods God brought me through. I thank God for all the blessings and miracles manifested in my life. In spite of what I have been through, I know that I am a child of God, and I still have joy.

Chapter Two

The Context of My Ministry

New Prospect Missionary Baptist Church was originally established in Detroit, Michigan in 1924. It was organized by a few officers and members of Mount Beulah Baptist Church. This small group banded together and first organized a church that they named Mount Lebanon Baptist Church. Two ministers, Rev. Talbert and Rev. Smith, worked together in the organization of the church. This small faithful group of people purchased a lot at 20470 Wisconsin in Detroit. More people moved into the area and joined Mount Lebanon Baptist Church. The name was changed to First Baptist Church.

Reverend Smith served as pastor until sometime in 1931. Reverend Theodore Williams served the remainder of 1931 until 1935. During his pastorate, he embraced new teachings that caused much confusion among the membership. Rev. Williams left First Baptist, taking deacons and members with him to organize another church. First Baptist was left without a pastor. The church later called Rev. Samuel Pyles who served about three years and started to rebuild the congregation of First Baptist. He also started renovations on the church building. God called Rev. Pyles from labor to reward in 1938. He died before he was able to finish the renovations. His assistant, Rev. Sandy Gibson, carried out his term and served for a short while until his death in 1939.

Reverend Charles B. Heath was called as pastor in the spring of 1939. Much was accomplished under Reverend Heath's administration. Due to the fact that there were two churches in Detroit with the same name, Reverend Heath had the church change its name from First Baptist to New Prospect Missionary Baptist Church on January 7, 1945.

In 1953 the church voted to enlarge their existing building. The members supported this effort and contributed considerably. In March 1960, they borrowed ten thousand dollars and made the down payment to purchase a building at 6330 Pembroke. Reverend Heath pastored the church for twenty-eight years until his death in 1967.

In February 1968, the church called Reverend Dr. Samuel Leon Whitney from Jackson, Mississippi to pastor the church. Under his pastoral leadership, the facilities were expanded to its current structure, which includes an eight hundred seat sanctuary, fellowship hall with multipurpose rooms, full-service kitchen, finance room, nursery and a new pastor's office. Under his leadership, the church was able to pay off the mortgage and purchase three houses. There was much growth under Rev. Whitney until his death in December 1990. His son, Reverend Dr. Keith L. Whitney assumed the pastoral leadership from 1991 until 1996. Reverend Randolph F. Henlon, who was the assistant pastor at the time, served as interim pastor from 1996 until March 1999.

New Growth

On March 1, 1999, history was made at New Prospect and in Detroit. A female was elected the senior pastor of New Prospect Missionary Baptist Church. I have always loved New Prospect Missionary Baptist Church, I just didn't know who they were. I confess that I was not interested in being the pastor of any church. I was very content being an effective assistant pastor to Dr. Charles G. Adams. When I dismissed the idea on my own, I decided that perhaps I should take this matter to the Lord. I asked the Lord one question: What shall I do about New Prospect Missionary Baptist Church? The Lord replied, "They don't want you, but they need you. Put in your application."

Prior to submitting my application, New Prospect Missionary Baptist Church had contacted me about being their Women's Day speaker for September, 1998. I declined because of a previous commitment. The Lord made sure that I graced the pulpit of New Prospect Missionary Baptist Church as the first female pastoral candidate, not just another Women's Day speaker.

I faced several challenges when I assumed the role of pastor of New Prospect. My administrative offices were inadequate due to the tremendous increase in membership. At that time, the administrative offices were located around the corner on Livernois Avenue, in a building owned by New

Prospect. They needed to be on the premises of the actual church building. There was also a lack of classrooms for Bible study and Sunday school classes. In order to handle our growth, we needed to first optimize the use of our existing space.

After surveying the property, I discovered that the old sanctuary and fellowship hall were not being utilized to their fullest. God revealed a new vision to me. I began to unfold to the church the vision of new administrative offices and six new multipurpose rooms. This involved renovating the entire old church building and sanctuary. It was an expensive and timely project. We moved into the newly renovated building in June 2001.

Catching God's Vision

New Prospect Missionary Baptist Church is made up of tithers, sacrificial givers and those who give offerings. I look forward to the ways the Lord will reveal to me how to encourage my congregation to give Him their all—time, talents and treasures—in order to move the church forward.

I understand the critical part the pastor plays in the process of articulating, interpreting and lifting up the significance of God's vision on the life of both the pastor and the congregation. Proverbs 29:18 declares that the church will perish without a vision. New Prospect Missionary Baptist Church believes that God is working in us, and His plans are beyond anything we could ask, think or imagine. It is a church that has been empowered for the future.

In the book, *Leading the Congregation*, Norman Shawchuck and Roger Heuser characterize church growth by describing three types of churches: the wishing, dreaming and visionary churches. According to the authors, in the wishing church, things remain the same. There is no evidence of change. No one really expects wishes to come true. This attitude generates irresponsible actions, no efforts or anything positive. A wishing church does a lot of talking, and "then excuse themselves from any responsibility to change" (Shawchuck and Heuser 1993, 141).

Although somewhat different from the wishing church, the dreaming church covers its wishes with emotions. A dreaming church uses their energy "pining over their dreams" (Shawchuck and Heuser 1993, 142), but when it comes to making the dream work, they have no energy left. Dreaming churches lack commitment. Some congregations, the authors write, "dream the future by dwelling on the past" (Shawchuck and Heuser 1993, 142). Dreaming churches know how to cry, scream and respond, but they remain the same when it is time to work. Dreaming churches are paralyzed by thinking that it is just too good to be true.

The third kind of church is a visionary church. Congregations possessed by a vision from God are instinctively different from wishers or dreamers (Shawchuck and Heuser 1993, 142). I have watched the vision that God has planned for New Prospect capture the very hearts of the people. Their spirits are alive. Their conviction is that God can do the impossible with us and through us, so they make sacrifices for the future.

Shawchuck and Heuser quote Episcopal priest, Terry Fullam, who defines vision as "the product of God working in us. God creates the vision and we receive it; it becomes a rallying point, a goal toward which we move as God's people" (1993, 144). New Prospect Missionary Baptist Church is a church that wants to accomplish great things for the Lord. Thus, we keep our eyes open to see God move and our ears open to hear Him speak.

As the leader of a visionary church, I must lead my congregation into a deeper spiritual walk with the Lord. I must teach them to listen to what the Spirit is saying to the church as we fit together to make the vision come true. In our church, Jesus is the Head, the Holy Spirit is the Guide and the pastor is the under shepherd. We have a church covenant that governs our actions. The Church Covenant can be found in Appendix A.

New Prospect Missionary Baptist Church has many ministries. These ministries serve and meet the needs of the church and community. For example, the Deacon and Deaconess Ministries help the pastor meet the spiritual needs of the church. They are responsible for the prepara- tion and serving of our Holy Communion. They prepare for our Baptism service and they care for the candidates. The Trustee Ministry is responsible for the accurate accounting of our finances and they oversee our church properties.

The Christian Education Ministry is responsible for the spiritual growth of the body of Christ. This includes Sunday School, Bible seminars, conferences, mid-week education classes, prayer meetings, and so forth. The General Mission and Family Life Ministries support our outreach ministries e.g., Meals on Wheels and food and clothing drives to help the community and our ministry to the homeless. What a privilege it is to bring joy into someone's life!

The Courtesy and Usher Ministries welcome our new members and visitors. The Bereavement and Support groups provide comfort and care. Finally, the Music Ministries consist of a Women's Choir, Handbell Choir, Y.A.M. Choir (Young Adults in Ministry), Youth and Children's Celestial Choir, Mighty Men of God Male Chorus, and the Choraleers Gospel Choir. The Music Ministry enhances the worship services by leading the congregation in singing and offering praises to our God. There are many other ministries that are very much involved in the life of the ministry of the church.

Christ is the Good, Great and Chief Shepherd. The pastor is the under shepherd, and the people are the sheep. I understand that I am to feed, keep, edify, encourage, protect and help the sheep with patience and much love. I believe that in order to care for God's people, pastoral leaders need the same tools that Jesus demonstrated: obedience, humility, love, accountability, faithfulness and a desire to grow. With determination and these tools, you will develop a leadership system that will equip and guard the service of ministry.

Chapter Three

The Leadership Style of Jesus

Jesus was so effective in His ministry. People were drawn into His ministry because they were attracted to Jesus. Listen to this invitation:

> Come to me, all you that are weary and are carrying heavy burdens, and I will give you rest. Take my yoke upon you, and learn from me; for I am gentle and humble in heart, and you will find rest for your souls. For my yoke is easy, and my burden is light. (Matthew 11:28–30).

Jesus' spirituality is a model for all leaders. After careful study, Shawchuck and Heuser preferred to call Jesus' spiritual disciplines "spiritual delights." According to these authors, all leaders should embrace these three elements of Jesus' spirituality (1993, 46–47):

1. Jesus carried out His ministry within the context of a small, intimate, covenant community.
2. Jesus established a rhythm of public ministry and private time.
3. Jesus taught by example that six graces were vital to His life and ministry.

Jesus established private time around public ministry. He would move from public ministry to prayer time, from prayer to public ministry. Jesus always found time to be alone with God.

Jesus used six *graces* that were vital to His life and ministry. *Prayer* was important to Jesus, and it must be important to those who lead in ministry. *Fasting* was important to Jesus so He would be prepared for the work. *The Lord's Supper* was important to Him, for it was a healing and restoring meal. Scripture teaches us that our Lord ate with His community often. Jesus taught the *Scriptures* with authority. He had a way of opening minds with God's Word as no other teacher. Jesus had many *conversations* where He shared His spirituality with others. Finally, Jesus *worshipped* regularly, and proclaimed His message in the synagogues.

From Jesus, we learn to wait upon God for effective ministry. Our busy and fast-paced society might consider waiting a waste of time. However, when we wait on God, we shall renew our strength. We may run and not be weary; and walk and not faint (Isaiah 40:31).

I am attracted to Jesus because of His life and His words. The message that love, forgiveness, redemption, grace and mercy is extended to all is attractive. The message that Jesus offers something that the world cannot offer is also attractive. In the book, *Jesus on Leadership*, C. Gene Wilkes, sought to understand Jesus' leadership style. His observations led to his sharing seven principles of servant leadership, which are:

- Humble your heart.
- First, be a follower.
- Find greatness in service.
- Take risks.
- Take up the towel.
- Share responsibility and authority.
- Build a team.

We see the life of Jesus in all four Gospels. We see Him being humble and totally centered on God's purposes. In coming to know Jesus, I was particularly amazed by two things about Him. The first was that Jesus loved me. Then, I was amazed that He wanted to be my best friend. That is the same message I give to my congregation. I want to help people know who Jesus is. I want them to be attracted to Jesus; not the messenger. It is worthy to note that Jesus attracted many people by simply saying, "Follow Me."

I want people to be attracted to New Prospect Missionary Baptist Church because they feel at home and see the love of God and Jesus there. I want New Prospect to be a place where we encourage and care for one another. I want New Prospect Missionary Baptist Church to be a place where the teaching is relevant and challenging, so families can grow. I also want it to reflect the Spirit of Jesus—His humility and service to others. One of the ways I demonstrate Jesus' humble service is by personally washing the feet of our Deacons during their ordination service.

Jesus came to earth to reach people. He brought answers to their questions. Jesus loved people, and He could be trusted. Jesus offered freedom and eternal life. In *Growing Leaders by Design*, Harold L. Longenecker states, "Jesus actively called people to follow, and so must we. Jesus attracted followers by teaching, preaching, healing and ministering" (1995, 143). Throughout the book, Longenecker challenges leaders to call people to form relationships, grow and envision the future.

Jesus was committed to developing souls. Longenecker stated:

> Jesus required His disciples to undergo a full range of disciplines in the company of fellow strugglers, under the authority of His Word, and with His confirming presence. Jesus' concerns went way beyond skills and programs or methods or even ministry excellence. He was growing people who would know Him and know themselves and would thus be able to know and nurture others (1995, 54).

Longenecker went on to say, that effective Christian leaders are marked by faith, growth, relationships and vision (1995, 73), but suggested that those nouns be substituted by four dynamic verbs: commit, change, connect and concentrate. He suggests that if we do this, we will attract people as Jesus did.

Commit to Prayer

One method I use to attract people is my commitment to a lifestyle of prayer. The church cannot miss opportunities to embrace prayer and to witness about faith. I am committed to convincing my congregation that all members of our church family need prayer because prayer brings about unity.

> *How very good and pleasant it is when kindred live together in unity! It is like precious oil on the head, running down upon the beard, on the beard of Aaron, running down over the collar of his robes. It is like the dew of Hermon, which falls on the mountains of Zion. For there the Lord ordained his blessing, life forevermore (Psalm 133).*

I am committed to making New Prospect Missionary Baptist Church the church where the spirit of unity abides.

Although we live in a world that struggles with sin and selfishness, we must encourage one another to pray. I believe that people need the church. People need a relationship with God. People need to come together, and they need to come to a place where a relationship with God and each other is stressed and encouraged.

Change and Grow

Longenecker writes that we are in the people-changing business (1995, 144). We must encourage people to get involved in the life of the church, to change and to grow. By increasing the Christian education opportunities at New

Prospect, I have seen appetites develop and increase for the Word of God. I have seen a renewed atmosphere of prayer and a hunger to bring the unsaved to church.

Jesus talked about the seed in the Gospels. The seed becomes a plant. The plant grows, and then there is a harvest. Paul told the Corinthians that God uses one person to plant a seed and another to water it, but only God gives the increase (I Corinthians 3:6). I know that New Prospect Missionary Baptist Church has attained certain heights, but there is more. I know New Prospect has experienced depths, but there is more. I know New Prospect has traveled distances, but there is more. So as we grow and move toward our destination of loving God and each other, God will give the increase and a transformation will take place.

Connect with Others

I share with all my members that I look forward to their becoming a part of the life of the church. There must be a willingness to connect with other believers. "It produces a climate in which people can discover a new dimension" in life (Longenecker 1995, 145). It takes people working together to make the vision a reality.

In the Bible, Christians are referred to as fellows: fellow workers, fellow citizens, fellow soldiers. We change and grow by being concerned for one another, by appreciating one another and by loving one another. I receive much joy from my relationships with other people. There is great joy in being connected.

Concentrate on God's Work

Jesus concentrated on the work God gave Him to do. As a pastor, I must concentrate on equipping my congregation to witness and communicate the Gospel. I must concentrate on developing a hunger within their spirits to seek the Lord. I must concentrate on promoting community involvement. I believe that there is a new way of leading, attracting and following. It is being a community that makes a difference.

In *Ministry Formation for Effective Leadership,* William R. Nelson, introduces three biblical models of pastoral leadership: Peter, Stephen and Paul. Each helps pastors/leaders discover their uniqueness. Peter made working with people central. Stephen was satisfied with developing programs. Paul found a balance between people and performance.

Peter's story can be found in Paul's letters, the book of Acts, the four Gospels and Peter's letters. Peter was a preacher and miracle worker who received guidance from heaven. God prepared Peter so he would listen to God. God knew Peter would need to listen to Him as he moved into a new Gentile mission (Acts 10:9–16).

Peter was prepared for personal relationships, and it did not matter if they were with Jews or Gentiles. He knew how to encourage people with whom he came in contact. Nelson writes:

> His strength emerged from the center of his being, rather than from the outward accomplishments of his doing. His natural leadership style found expression in openness to those in

need, regardless of their nationality or ethnic backgrounds (Nelson 1988, 49).

Stephen's story is found only in the Book of Acts. Stephen was full of wisdom, faith and the Holy Spirit. He engaged in ministry and enabled the other apostles to pray and study the Word. Stephen performed great wonders and miracles, all of which met with opposition. He had a "tell it like it is" leadership style, which eventually led to his death. Yet, Stephen's martyrdom also led to the spreading of the Gospel throughout Judea and Samaria. Nelson states:

> Stephen's single focus on confronting and changing the Jewish captivity of the early church may be described as an efficient, though costly, leadership style. The task was accomplished, even though he did not survive to receive praise for launching the early church on its world mission (Nelson 1988, 55).

Paul's story is found in his own letters and the Book of Acts. Paul worked with people, and he had goals. Paul was able to identify his past and create his future. And it all started with one transforming moment in his life. Although Paul had effectively persecuted the early believers, he effectively evangelized the world. His people-leadership style is seen during his three missionary journeys and a trip to Rome, where he effectively preached, but not without struggles. Paul totally depended on God. Through transformation of the Holy Spirit, he became God's person, doing God's will.

Nelson suggests that if, like Peter the reformed priest, you have the gift of working with people, you are an empathetic leader. If you have the gift of administration, like Stephen the confrontative prophet, you are an efficient leader. If persistent like Paul, who represented a kingly missionary, you are an effective leader. Peter represents the past, Stephen represents the present and Paul represents the future. Effective leadership is always in the process of coming from the past, of working through the present and going to the future (Nelson 1988, 64).

Jesus is the Head of the church, and the Holy Spirit is the Director. The Holy Bible is a leader's highest standard of authority for help and guidance. The Lord needs pastors and people who are determined to follow leadership and carry out their ministries with their hearts and minds.

The church needs people who are willing to use all their strength to perform their God-given responsibilities. We need people who are more determined to produce results. Jesus expects us to submit to His authority and to the authority of the church in order to win souls for Christ. A Christ-centered system of leadership will teach discipline, focus on the vision daily and keep all things in order.

Chapter Four

A Good Steward of Spiritual Joy

W hat does it mean to be a good steward of spiritual joy? I believe that as a Christian and a steward, I am expected to manage well that which God has given me. I am to manage my time, talents and treasures. It is my understanding that we are not to use our resources to satisfy our own desires, but we should use them as tools to carry on the work of God's kingdom.

Everything we own belongs to God. The Lord loves a joyful giver. If this is true, and I believe that it is, then I must use my resources to help carry on God's ministry in this world. I must respond to God's people who are in need, and I must do it joyfully, for when I minister to others, I am ministering to Christ.

Giving Back to God

I am a Christian and in obedience to God's Word, I tithe. I tithe over and above a tenth of my income. I give my time, my energy, my care and compassion to the people whom God loves. All that I possess is available for God's use in the work of the kingdom. I decided that I did not want to miss out on the full, rich blessings that God has for me because of my disobedience. I feel that I dishonor my covenant with God when I am disobedient. I believe I forfeit unknown blessings when I do not obey the Word of God. Therefore, not only am I a tither, I am a sacrificial giver. And I lead my congregation by example. I give back to the Lord without a shadow of a doubt that God will take care of me. I also know that whatever I give cannot compare to God's provision for me. My giving demonstrates my faith, gratefulness and trust in God.

It is important that the church give back to God by finding ways of giving back to the community. We are to feed the hungry, clothe the naked, give water to the thirsty, welcome strangers, and visit the sick and those in prison. We can share our wealth by adopting a needy family, ministering to veterans, supporting a homeless shelter, or financially supporting college students, just to name a few.

The church is the channel through which Christ does His work. Our support of the church and its ministries reflects the depth of our belief in what Christ desires to accomplish through His church. Great faith produces generous giving. Our generous God is looking for a generous church. My constant prayer is that God will look upon the New Prospect Missionary Baptist Church as an example of His generosity in our dealings with others. (A list of our charitable donations to other ministries, organizations and those in need can be found in Appendix B.)

I have found my stewardship to be a joyful, great blessing for me. God has been generous to me in so many ways. Proverbs 22:9 says, *"Those who are generous are blessed."* I am never more like God than when I give, and God continues to lavish grace upon my family.

I consider it a significant privilege and honor to be a part of the Christian ministry. I belong to Christ. I follow and I live for Christ. My devotion and obedience is real and complete. My allegiance cannot be divided. I know I am unworthy. Therefore, I dedicate all I have—time, talents, money and power of body, soul and spirit—to the service of Christ.

The Reason for My Joy

My call into ministry was more than a call; it was a commandment. There was no time for consideration. My mind was made up, and my decision was settled, just like my grandmother had said. I can still remember that Sunday in June 1974. Sunday evening worship service was always high in the Spirit. I must admit that I was quite satisfied singing in the choir and ushering in my tight, white uniform. But out of all the women present that night, young and old, God called me. God chose me!

I had just finished singing my favorite solo, "If the Lord Wants Somebody, Here am I! Send Me!" I knew in my heart that if my mother wouldn't go and if my father couldn't go, I would certainly go anywhere and do anything for the Lord. I was caught up in something that I cannot fully explain even now. I heard the Lord speak! I felt the Lord near! God spoke into the very depths of my soul and called forth something that was there all the time. The Lord told me to go and preach the Gospel and minister joyously to His people. Since that day, I have not been the same. I have made a liar out of Satan and all the others who thought my calling would not last. For you see, I tried everything: men, jobs, school and nothing worked for me. Since that day when God hired me, I have stayed on the battlefield, and everyday I can say, "I'm not the same anymore."

I will never forget September 15, 1974, at Mt. Olive Baptist Church in East Orange, New Jersey. I preached my trial sermon and received my license to preach the gospel. The Lord has shaped and molded me for ministry for over thirty years. I am the proud wife of a deacon and the mother of two sons, and it is a privilege to participate in shaping their lives as well. I have been anointed with power and gifts to impact the lives of others. I am able to move and persuade people, and I just want the Lord to use me! I can't thank God enough for calling me into the ministry.

I treasure His anointing and I operate in it to minister to His people. His Spirit is manifested in me in the hospital rooms, as I tell the sick that the life-giving power of the Holy Spirit belongs to them. His Spirit is seen in me when I visit the sick in their homes, hugging our senior citizens, touching our shut-in members and sharing the message that companionship with the living Christ is real. God's anointing helps me when counseling our children about life and death.

I call on His presence at every funeral by preaching comfort and hope from the Scriptures. Yes, I love and cherish my calling, and I know that this is where I am supposed to be right now.

Pastor Carl Johnson, a friend in the ministry, says, "There is much talk about the Jezebels of history, and how their manipulative powers have swept people off their feet and ruled their every move." I certainly agree. Jezebel was beautiful, ambitious and eager to share the throne with a king. She had ways of seducing others. She was wicked and certainly persuasive. She possessed gifts, and she was not an ordinary woman. But all of her powers flowed in the wrong direction. Should we not talk more about the Hannahs, Lydias, Priscillas and Marys of the world? Hannah was a devoted mother. She was prayerful even when she was childless. Lydia was a successful businesswoman and still found time to worship the Lord. Priscilla was content and connected to her Christ and her husband. Mary Magdalene gave her best to the Master. I see and feel so much of myself in all of these women.

Reverend Pearl Sterling from Texas said, "Much is said about the woman at the well, but too little is said about the woman who left the well." I stand proud that I am one of the women who left the well. I finally found someone who really wanted me. I came to the well with all of my baggage, and the Lord launched me into the world with my joy. The Lord sent me into the world, unannounced and without theological training, but anointed to compel men, women, boys and girls to come see a man, who told me all things that ever I did, a man who still wanted me! So I don't mind sharing my story, especially with the unsaved and discouraged children of God.

I am so glad that Jesus offered me the plan of salvation. I discovered a better way, the only way, and I cannot keep it to myself. I will not keep it to myself! I must minister, teach and preach the Gospel that saves. I must do it because many are still lost and some are not aware of their lost state. But they need to know that there is a better way. They need to know that their state of being lost need only be a temporary condition. This entire world is lost, but Jesus came to find those who are lost.

I can look back on my life and say that my accepting the call into the Christian ministry was the turning point in my life. Joy and light took over. The crisis passed. I waved my troubles good-bye, and healing took place. It was like stepping onto an elevator going down and finding myself going up. I know that Jesus snatched me from a junk pile, crowned me to be a teacher and a preacher and filled me with His joy. I know now that nothing can defeat God. He is with me and the Spirit in me gives me the faith to rise up, press forward and meet any challenge without fear. When fear comes, I stop and pray, trusting God for divine direction and guidance. I know God is the power at work in my world. He is the power at work in the lives of my loved ones and in me. I am not the same anymore! And that is why I have joy! Praises to my God!

What Does God Require?

Micah 6:8 speaks to every minister, especially to me, and asks the question, *"What does the Lord require of you?"* This is a question we all have to answer. It is a theological question because we live in God's world. To find life's meaning, I must find out what God wants of me.

Micah 6:8 goes on to answer this question by saying that it is *"to do justice, and to love kindness, and to walk humbly with God."* To do justice is to do the right thing. I must do wrong to none, and do right to all. To love mercy is to love kindness. It is remembering that there are people who are having some hard times. So I must be kind and show mercy to all who may need me to help them or give them some love. To walk humbly with God is to accept God's offer of grace, give Him reverence and live in the light of His love.

What does the Lord require of me? I am to conform to the will of God, maintain communion with God, and study to show myself approved unto God. By conforming to the will of God, all of us, men and women, can answer the question: What does the Lord require of me?

What does the Lord require of me? Steadfastness in doing His will. It hasn't been easy, and I don't expect that to change. By the strength of the Spirit of God dwelling within me, I am assured of my position. A woman can be a Christian minister/pastor in the midst of, and in spite of, opposing circumstances. I know for myself that greater is the One that is in me, than the one who is in the world (I John 4:4 NIV). Although it is not easy, it is possible as long as I act justly, love mercifully and walk humbly with God. My journey in ministry is possible only when God truly dwells within me.

My Joyful Mission

My call has given me a joyful mission. I am on a mission to tell the world about God the Father, God the Son and God the Holy Spirit. There is only one true and living God. He is my Creator, Redeemer, Preserver and Ruler of the universe. I owe God the highest love, reverence and obedience.

I am on a mission for Jesus, and I am happy with Jesus alone. I know the Lord personally, intimately and He is the source of my joy. This joy goads my mission to tell the world about a Physician who understands all diseases and can heal all diseases. Men and women are universally in a diseased state of unbelief; ignorant of God and the gospel; having hardened heads and hearts; and trusting in their own right-eousness and hypocrisy, just to name a few.

I must share my joy and tell every man, woman, boy and girl about the healing, saving presence of Christ. I must tell everyone about the operation of the Holy Spirit, the divine Word, and teach them the meaning of the ordinances—the Lord's Supper and Baptism. I must also tell them about the power of prayer and the influence of other saints.

My mission includes joyfully telling the world that Jesus Christ is the eternal Son of God. God, in His incarnation as Jesus Christ, was conceived of the Holy Spirit and born of the Virgin Mary. Jesus perfectly revealed and did the will of

God. He came into the world to be the sacrificial lamb for my sins, and I know it. Sin had separated and broken fellowship with God and humans. Therefore, Jesus came to reconcile the world to God. Although Jesus took upon Himself the demands and necessities of human nature, and the sins of the world, He never sinned.

Joyfully, my mission is to tell the world that Jesus died an atoning death on the Cross. He died on Calvary for the remission of my past, present and future sins and I must tell somebody. I must tell the story that Jesus is the Son of God with power to save by His resurrection from the dead. For Jesus is both the crucified Savior and the living Lord. I want the Holy Spirit to use me to awaken unbelievers to their need for Christ and encourage believers to continue holding on to Christ, no matter what.

Though joyful, I am serious about this mission I am on and the battle I am in. I am in a battle, but it is not with or against my brothers and sisters. It is against the world, the flesh and Satan.

Chapter Five

The Psalmist Model of Spiritual Joy

I believe that the Bible supports my joyful ministry style. When I think about "giving away my joy," I think about David and his music, which inevitably leads me to the Book of Psalms. In I Samuel 16, we find that evil spirits fled when David played his harp. The writer, who would later record the Psalms, had the joy of music in him, and the Bible says in I Samuel 16:18, "the Lord was with him."

I have the Lord and music in me, and that combination produces joy. Music is a gift from God, and I am enjoying my gift. Robert C. Anderson stated in his book, *The Effective Pastor* (1985, 324), "Music is a supreme gift from God able to inspire, to bless, and to thrill man in a way no other art can."

I believe that the Holy Spirit has anointed me to "give away my joy" through the combination of proclaiming the preached Word, hearing the Lord speak and making music. I do not entertain, but worship and give God glory and thanks in all that I do. I consider myself a psalmist leader, and therefore have established a paradigm called the Psalmist Model of Spiritual Joy, based on the teachings of the Psalms.

There are five scriptural steps that explain what I consider the commitment of a psalmist leader who follows my model of spiritual joy.

1. **A psalmist pastoral leader delights in participating in God's unfolding drama of redemption as a suffering servant.** *"For His anger is but for a moment, His favor is for life; Weeping may endure for a night, But joy comes in the morning" (Psalm 30:5 NKJV).* There is nothing more difficult to accept or understand than those times in a Christian's life where we must submit ourselves to the discipline of suffering or to the correcting hand of God. But the beauty and comfort of our relationship with Him is in knowing that these moments, although difficult, will be brief, especially in comparison to the everlasting love and favor that God has towards us. Following these moments of weeping is promised joy. When you consider the Hebrew word used here, *rinnah*, the crying actually continues, but it goes from weeping to gladness. *Rinnah* means "a shout of joy or grief."

   It is interesting to note that in the African-American church, crying and shouting are done both in times of sadness and joy. I am prone to shout out in moments of desperation, just as I am in times of thanksgiving and adulation. My ultimate comfort comes from knowing that God's merciful redemption is forever unfolding and being extended to me, despite how dark my days may be. This is truly a song for the redeemed; knowing that we can celebrate trial, test or trauma, and the release of God's peace and presence into our lives in the same manner.

2. **A psalmist pastoral leader delights in shouting for joy.**

"But let all those rejoice who put their trust in You; Let them ever shout for joy, because You defend them; Let those also who love Your name Be joyful in You."
(Psalm 5:11 NKJV).

It is not unusual for one to express joy with a shout, a loud exclamation of satisfaction or appreciation to God or others for something favorable. The Hebrew word, *ranan*, means "to shout for joy, to give a ringing cry." When we love God and recognize that He defends us against the adversary and all those who come against us, it is a natural and comfortable response to shout for joy. As pastor, I do not withhold my emotions. I need to cry out or shout when expressing my gratitude for God's mercy and kindness demonstrated to me and my church. I want my church family to see that I am moved by the hand of God, humbled by His loving kindness and willing to show my appreciation at all times. Therefore, I delight in shouting for joy.

3. **A psalmist pastoral leader delights in trusting God as a refuge.**

"But let all who take refuge in you rejoice; let them ever sing for joy. Spread your protection over them, so

*that those who love your name may
exult in you." (Psalm 5:11).*

Perhaps the most common of the Hebrew words for
joy is *simchah*, which means "gladness; mirth; to
rejoice and be glad." We are encouraged by the
psalmist, David, to rejoice in the fact that we can trust
in God, knowing that He will defend and shelter us. In
these times of uncertainty about terrorists attacks
and insecurity of our homeland security, it is
comforting to know that in spite of our dependence
upon the intelligence agencies of our country, our
allies, and our military strength, God is our refuge and
He is the only sure-proof and rock-solid place in
which we know that we are safe. Psalm 91:9–10 says,
*"because we have made him our refuge...there shall
no evil befall us."* It is important for me to live,
preach and teach my church family that our assurance in the sheltering presence of God is the greatest
insurance that we could have. Therefore, we trust in
God, and this trust brings us joy.

4. **A psalmist pastoral leader delights in triumphing over
the enemy.** *"Oh, clap your hands, all you peoples!
Shout to God with the voice of triumph!" (Psalm
47:1 NKJV).* The Hebrew word used to describe the
shout of triumph is *ruwa*. It is also a signal for war or
a march against the enemy. It represents a great and
joyful noise. A songwriter penned, "Don't wait until the
battle is over, shout now!" This shout would be

similar to the Israelites' shout when they marched around the walls of Jericho, knowing that their enemies were about to be defeated at their hands.

I must encourage my people to shout with the voice of triumph as an act of faith, knowing that God has already defeated our enemies. We must shout with joy in triumph because God's Word is true when it says, *"the battle is not yours but God's"* *(II Chronicles 20:15)*. We must make a joyful noise and shout in triumph because *"greater is He that is in us than he that is in the world"* *(I John 4:4)*. Regardless of the enemies that may confront me, I will make a joyful noise unto the Lord!

5. **A psalmist pastoral leader delights in the mercy of God.** *"I will be glad and rejoice in Your mercy, For You have considered my trouble; You have known my soul in adversities"* *(Psalm 31:7 NKJV)*. I wish there were stronger words to describe what I feel about knowing God's mercy in my life. The fact that it is free and unlimited brings me to a point of overflowing joy and my deepest feelings of appreciation are not adequately expressed. David chose the Hebrew word, *samach*, in this text to describe the joy and gladness that he felt in having the mercy of God in times of trouble. I cannot help but consider how merciful God has been to me during the times when I was caught up in trouble and adversities, many of which were brought on by my own hand. It was

because God knew my soul, my entire being, and had chosen me for His work, long before I chose Him, that He was so merciful to me. I live by and through God's mercies, today. I rejoice that they are *"new every morning,"* for without them, I would be consumed.

Implementing the Psalmist Model

The first sermon I preached as a candidate for the pastorate of New Prospect Missionary Baptist Church was "The Joy of the Lord Is My Strength." God introduced my pastoral/ministry leadership style to the congregation from the very beginning.

My Psalmist Model of Spiritual Joy has given New Prospect Missionary Baptist Church many things. This unique style has changed the church forever. Publicity and accolades caused the Detroit News to call us the "fastest growing Baptist church in the Detroit metropolitan area."

> *Then the one who had received the five talents came forward, bringing five more talents, saying, "Master, you handed over to me five talents; see, I have made five more talents." His master said to him, "Well done, good and trustworthy slave; you have been trustworthy in a few things, I will put you in charge of many things; enter into the joy of your master"* (Matthew 25:20–21).

In the parable of the talents, I see one who was faithful becoming the leader over many and entering into the joy of his master by giving away his joy. Since entering into the joy of the Lord, the Lord has been preparing me to do ministry with joy. The Lord has rewarded me with the great responsibility of pastoring a church where I can give away my joy. In doing so, I have developed the Psalmist Model of Spiritual Joy as a five-fold paradigm, which consists of the following principles:

I. Focus on joy and gratitude rather than problems.

When I became the senior pastor of New Prospect Missionary Baptist Church, people wanted to interview me and talk with me about the problem many had with a woman pastor. I declined because all I wanted to talk about was the joy of being in ministry.

Dr. Charles G. Adams, pastor of Hartford Memorial Baptist Church and past president of the Progressive National Baptist Convention, Inc., wrote in my first anniversary booklet, "All the rejected stones and oppressed people in the world can look at Pastor Wilma Johnson and take courage!" Dr. E. L. Branch, pastor of Third New Hope Baptist Church and past president of the Baptist Missionary Educational State Convention of Michigan and the Council of Baptist Pastors, wrote, "You are a valuable asset to the kingdom of God. God rewards the kind of faithfulness you so vividly demonstrate. Your spirit is the kind that patiently insists upon progress and aggressively works to make things happen." For over five years, the Psalmist Model of Spiritual Joy has been used at New Prospect. The transformation has been tremendous. While it is, at times, unbelievable to us, we are not surprised by what God does. Praise God!

II. Introduce new, meaningful and vibrant worship services.

New, meaningful and vibrant worship services have brought new life and joy to New Prospect. Since the first Sunday I preached as pastor-elect, the services have been overflowing. The multitude just keeps coming. The worship services are exciting and full of the energy of the Holy Spirit.

I would like to share a few things that happened in the first year of giving away my joy.

- Welcomed five hundred thirteen (513) new members
- Baptized one hundred sixty (160)
- Started Wednesday Bible Study and Power Wednesday Worship and Prayer services at 11:00 a.m. and 6:00 p.m.
- Established Lenten Family Journey
- Added 6:00 a.m. Easter Resurrection Sunrise Service
- Held our first revival conducted by the late Reverend Dr. Frederick G. Sampson
- Established a $1 million Endowment Fund
- Established the New Prospect Optimist Club
- Began radio advertisements

Some of the comments members shared with me at the end of my first year were:

- "Your presence has made a difference. The spirit is higher than it has been since we became members in 1973."
- "You've kept your promise by loving us, teaching us, and preaching God's Word."
- "You have the best hugs in the world next to Mama and Nana."
- "Thank you for bringing contentment to New Prospect Missionary Baptist Church for us all through Christ Jesus."
- "God has blessed New Prospect Missionary Baptist Church with a light that shines all the time."
- "Words cannot express how happy I am since you have been here with us. God answered our prayers and our request for a leader, and you are the one."
- "We love you and are truly inspired by your leadership."
- "We are blessed to have a pastor who cares. I admire and love you for enriching my life."
- "You have brought us back to a glorious new beginning. In one short year, you have built a Spirit-filled family."
- "My personal spiritual growth has been tremendous this past year. This has been a wonderful first year."

Since becoming the pastor of New Prospect Missionary Baptist Church, the membership and financial resources have increased tremendously. Our ability to help others has also increased, and I thank God for each opportunity to be a blessing to others.

III. Meet the special needs of special people.

It is important to me that New Prospect Missionary Baptist Church be a church home where everyone feels as if they are special and that their needs are accommodated. Some of our accomplishments in the second year of giving away my joy were:

- Welcomed four hundred eighty-eight (488) new members
- Baptized one hundred fifty-five (155)
- Celebrated our 1000th member
- Licensed the first females to preach the gospel at New Prospect Missionary Baptist Church
- Licensed the first females into the Deacon Ministry
- Paid off a $38,000 deficit for American Baptist College in Nashville, Tennessee
- Purchased a handicap van
- Adopted Pasteur Elementary School
- Awarded $36,000 in our annual scholarship, giving money from the principal of our endowment fund
- Established a Seasoned Senior Citizens Sunday in honor of our members who are sixty-five and over

IV. Be responsible, creative and explosive.

The creative ways I share my joy have not gone unnoticed by others. I realize that with joy comes responsibilities to the community we serve and to the world. Below are some things we achieved in the third year of giving away my joy.

- Established "At The Lighthouse Corporation," a community 501(c)(3) outreach ministry

- Welcomed five hundred six (506) new members
- Baptized one hundred eighty-seven (187)
- Began an after school program
- Moved into our new administrative offices (a $1 million project)

Seeking ways to joyfully build up the church, to edify and encourage the body of Christ, certainly occupies my time. Feeding the living Word of God to the people of God helps to promote their spiritual growth and maturity. Preparing the people of God to give service with joy to the community are also my goals. We must demonstrate that service with love and compassion. I want to enable the members to get involved in the ministries of the church.

V. Have a give and take relationship with your congregation.

I am striving to build meaningful relationships with my congregation. I have been given to the church to enhance their ability to do ministry among the believers. Therefore, when people fall, they see me picking them up. When someone fails, they see and hear me urging forgiveness and restoration. They constantly hear my cry to move on to greater accomplishments and higher ground in Christ Jesus.

In the Psalmist Model of Spiritual Joy, I strive to develop effective, meaningful relationships with the officers and people I love and serve. Michael E. Cavanagh writes in *The Effective Minister* that in order to be an effective pastor, I must be personal, caring and compassionate. This should stir up from the people feelings of trust, comfort and respect (1986, 17). He suggests that there are nine qualities an effective pastor should possess to some degree. He also suggests that an effective pastor must understand why these qualities are important. These qualities are:

1. **A Healthy Spirituality (Cavanagh 1986, 17)**

   An effective pastor must have an effective prayer life. Daily communication with the Lord, who is my power source, is crucial. "A prayer life," Cavanagh states, "is much more than saying prayers; it is a theme that permeates daily behaviors in significant, observable ways" (1986, 18). My personal prayer life has provided a foundation where I can stand, and continually find myself more patient and loving.

   Cavanagh suggests not only a prayer life, but also an assimilated theology. For example, it is not enough for me to know Psalm 23. I must know the Good Shepherd of Psalm 23. The deeper my growth, the deeper I can take my congregation.

2. **Helpful Motivation (Cavanagh 1986, 19)**

   An effective pastor must motivate, comfort and listen to others. "Problems occur," says Cavanagh, "when ministers give affection as an investment in order to seduce people into dependent relationships, to convert them to the minister's religious beliefs, to win their affection, or to own and control them" (1986, 20). This type of inspiration is not helpful.

Congregations should be drawn to their leaders because the leaders are drawn to Christ. When congregations are drawn to Christ, they will be drawn to each other. Whatever leaders receive from congregations, it should enhance their gifts and ability to better serve the Lord.

3. **Healthy Sensitivity (Cavanagh 1986, 24)**

An effective pastor must have the proper and true feelings to go along with the proper and true words.

> "Sensitivity is important in ministers because people often communicate their deepest concerns and feelings in veiled forms: an expression, a shift in posture, or a tightening of hands" (Cavanagh 1986, 24).

So many of our members are dealing with painful situations. When a young, unmarried woman reveals that she is pregnant, she does not need a lecture on having unprotected sex at that moment. What she needs is guidance, love and prayer to deal with the present. She needs someone to hold her and cry with her. Our congregations need sensitive leaders.

4. **Absolute Integrity and Honesty (Cavanagh 1986, 22)**

"Honesty means much more than simply not lying to people," writes Cavanagh. Since becoming the pastor of New Prospect, there have been several serious situations where I had to take firm action, and I had to be totally honest. It required courage and strength that only the Holy Spirit could give. I believe that I am able to minister freely because I know that I am not a liar or a thief. I can stand in my pulpit without feelings of guilt or shame because of any of my actions, known or unknown to others.

5. **Gentle Strength (Cavanagh 1986, 25)**

When an effective pastor declares Christian values from the pulpit, it must be done "with a gentleness that flows from genuine concern rather than from fear or anger; and with a strength that denotes commitment and conviction" (1986, 26). Even when my congregation frustrates me and causes discouragement, I must still find ways to communicate with them that are not harsh, but kind and productive.

6. **Genuinely Freeing (Cavanagh 1986, 27)**

As I lead my congregation along the path towards joy, I like to think that I have made them feel like they have the freedom to make choices. I can only attract people to follow Christ if my invitations are thoughtful and compassionate. I want a relationship with my congregation where they can say "no" to a request and still know that our relationship has not been broken or destroyed.

7. **Unconditionally Present (Cavanagh 1986, 30)**

This quality says that when a member strays, I will be there still ready to assist and to shine some light upon their pathways. Family, friends and other church members are too quick to condemn by their words and their actions. An effective pastor helps the person who has strayed to grow and live a Christian life after and in spite of having made foolish and irresponsible decisions in the past. Sometimes those very decisions cause much suffering and pain, altering lives forever. Cavanagh states, "Ministers do the psychological and spiritual resuscitation and leave the judging to God" (1986, 32).

8. Intellectually Competent (Cavanagh 1986, 32)

Effective pastors must be knowledgeable in order to carry out their responsibilities. They must have a willing spirit and a desire to always study and learn. "Competent ministers are intellectually growing," writes Cavanagh (1986, 32). The more I grow, the more I can help my congregation grow. Reading, attending workshops and conferences will motivate me to be creative. The information and energy that I receive provides me with knowledge and strength that is needed for my pastoral journey.

9. Approachability (Cavanagh 1986, 34)

I want my members to feel that they can contact me at any time. I want to be easy to talk to and open. I want to be approachable. With my arms wide open, I want my ministry to say, "Come closer." Cavanagh calls it being down-to-earth "so that anyone can understand, challenge and feel comfortable" (1986, 36) with me .

I am working toward the goal of being an effective pastoral minister. I want to be good for the souls of the people, and I need to possess the above qualities in order to do that. For I believe as Cavanagh states, "although not everyone needs a physician or a psychologist, everyone needs a pastoral minister" (1986, 37).

My tasks as the pastor are numerous: equip, educate, shepherd, lead, preach, teach, pray, love, correct, disciple, evangelize, pamper and care for the sheep. I want to communicate with the people I love while helping and touch their lives. When I became the pastor, I guaranteed the New Prospect Missionary Baptist Church family that I would teach, preach, love and pray. I promised them that I would always be prepared, and I have kept that promise. Everything else we have discovered by working together.

Giving Away My Joy

As my church family has continued to grow, it has been a personal challenge to ensure that the joy that I have is extended to each member. Because the membership of New Prospect Missionary Baptist Church is now more than three thousand people, it is impossible for me to touch each life on an individual, one-on-one basis all of the time. However, I recognize that it is important to make sure that my joy permeates our church and is felt by everyone who attends.

Obviously, because of the size of the congregation, my focus has had to be on sharing my joy spiritually, first, rather than physically. Because joy is indeed a spiritual experience,

I have been intent on increasing the spirituality of New Prospect Missionary Baptist Church. Henri L. Nouwen is quoted in *Leading the Congregation* as saying, "Spirituality is paying attention to the life of the spirit in us" (1993, 39).

I use six methods of giving my joy to my church family, five of which were verbalized by the authors of *The Door to Joy*, (Colorado Springs, CO: Relationship Resources, 1999) Ken L. Williams and Gaylyn Williams.

First, I embrace my church family with my words. Words are powerful. I always greet them with the words "Good morning, my family!" They like the way those words sound and feel. Yet, it is God's Word that reveals joy to them most. Therefore, my sermons are upbeat, positive and always reinforcing that we are loved, blessed and forgiven. It is the acceptance of those three things that brings joy to one's life despite the trials, tests or storms that come our way. The revelation I have received through those three things has given me joy, and I share my joy in teaching and speaking that to others.

*"God's Word **reveals** joy"* (Williams and Williams 1999, 25). I prepare and write sermons that speak to the needs of my congregation. I sing a song after every sermon that directly relates to the sermon topic. My church family loves to hear me sing and make the connection between the written Word and the words of the song. That's the psalmist in me. Music is a vital part of my life. It is a tool I use to spread God's joy to the world.

Secondly, I believe that *"prayer **maintains** joy"* (Williams and Williams 1999, 54) Therefore, I earnestly pray for my entire church family, within the worship service and outside. I encourage them to develop and sustain a prayer life. Spirituality is seen most in a praying church. To this end, we have intercessory prayer on Monday mornings, prayer service on Wednesday evenings before our Bible study class and Power Wednesday worship service, prayer retreats and times in which I call our leadership into hours of prayer. My church family knows that I am a praying pastor and they are able to see how it maintains my joy, and I share this joy with them through prayer.

I also believe that *"worship **unleashes** joy"* (Williams and Williams 1999, 63). So the third way in which I give my joy to my church family is through a powerful worship experience. Our services are spirit-filled and the people respond freely and express themselves in open praise that may result in shouting, dancing and bowed reverence to the Spirit of God. Oftentimes there are many who shed tears or openly weep at the release they feel in their hearts and spirits during our worship services. I have recognized that the spirit of the pastor determines in many ways the type of worship experience a church knows. Therefore, I ensure that our worship unleashes joy.

I always carefully watch my congregation. I fix my eyes upon their faces to see who is present of course, but mostly I want to see to whom the Holy Spirit will guide me so I can minister to them personally. There are times I will leave the pulpit and immediately give that person my undivided attention, or I will contact them later knowing they are in need. Hugs, tears, prayers and words of encouragement are definitely ways I give away my joy.

When people join the church, I personally talk to each person who comes into the family. I purposely take their right hand with my right hand so I can feel who they are. I have the gift of discernment and as the Holy Spirit guides, I love them in so many ways. They may start to cry, and sometimes I make it a private moment. When I need the church to participate in loving and praying with me for that individual, I will share.

I give Bibles to my children and teenagers, and to adults who need them. They are gifts from their new pastor. Then, I bow at the waist, in the presence of God and tell each of them, "It is my pleasure to serve as your pastor."

At the funeral worship services that I conduct, I always bring words of comfort from the Bible. It is a worship service of sharing the Gospel. There is a special time during the service when I ask the family members of the deceased to hug one another. I take the sadness and have them turn it into a moment of sharing love. I believe that when hugs are given, love is shared and some of the sadness is released. It is at this time that we always sing, "Victory and Joy is Mine." I then remind the family of the hope and joy that they have in God, even during their dark hour of bereavement.

Fourthly, I believe that *"friendship increases joy"* (Williams and Williams 1999, 82). I encourage the fellowshipping of the saints at New Prospect Missionary Baptist Church. On Wednesday afternoons, after our Bible Study and Power Wednesday worship service, lunch is prepared and served in our fellowship hall. This provides the church family with opportunities to share and get to know one another over a meal. We have other breakfasts, birthday celebrations or meal times, which are always free to our members, and are specifically designed to bring the church family together. In addition, there are dozens of ministries at New Prospect that offer occasions for relationship building. I believe that this increases the joy of the church family.

I also believe that *"giving and gratitude **encourage** joy"* (Williams and Williams 1999, 101). I have tried to set an example for giving in every way to my church family. I give freely to God, but I also give freely to them. It is done indiscriminately. I sponsor several members each year to attend the conferences we hold in conjunction with our Men's and Women's Day activities. I purchase tickets for various events and share them with the church family, especially faithful volunteers. I demonstrate my gratitude to them for the outpouring of love that they give to me and the church family. With regularity, I thank them for loving me, and I thank God for giving me the privilege of being their pastor.

God's Word in me, my prayer life, my love for worship, my appreciation for relationships and my belief in giving— all speak to my spirituality and to sharing these things, I give my joy to my church family.

The sixth way in which the three thousand members of New Prospect Missionary Baptist Church receive my joy is through my administrative and ministerial staff. I purposefully try to choose men and women who have my heart and spirit and who will share my joy in a manner in which they, too, will touch the lives of our church family. When I am unable to be physically present in the lives of the members, my spirit and my joy are definitely extended through my pastoral staff, ministers, deacons, deaconess, trustees and ministry chairs as well as my administrative, custodial and security staff.

For example, Reverend Dr. Craig D. Ester, Sr. serves as my Minister of Christian Education. I also depend on him for daily spiritual matters at the church. Reverend Ronald L. Copeland is my Minister of Administration. He spiritually oversees the physical plant, the adjoining properties and new building projects. Minister April Hearn is my Youth Minister, organizing and handling all activities that deal with our youth. Reverend Randolph Henlon is the Minister of Pastoral Care. He visits hospitals and nursing homes on a regular basis. Minister Doris Montgomery and Rev. Gary Pullum are my ministers of senior care. Their role is to nurture our seniors who are sixty-five and over, keeping me abreast of their concerns and needs. Minister Constance Garrett nurtures and cares for our young adults. My Deacon and Deaconess Ministries really touch the lives and spread my joy especially among the sick and shut-in family members. My other ministers assist me with pulpit duties and with the worship service. They also assist with our prison and nursing home ministries. It is my desire and belief that every member of New Prospect Missionary Baptist Church is a recipient of my joy. With the help of my staff and leadership team, I am able to ensure that every member is cared for with my joy.

There are other ways I give away my joy that mean a lot to my church family. I periodically mail out "hug" letters to our members. It never fails that members come to me to let me know the words came just when they needed them the most, and many desire to give me the hug that the letter requested of them. I read and respond in some way to every request placed in our Prayer Request Box. I mail out birthday cards to every member. I make many phone calls to my membership. I also respond to e-mail. I diligently try to ensure there is a feeling of a personal touch from the pastor for each member of New Prospect.

My congregation did not celebrate the seasons of Advent, Lent or Pentecost prior to my coming. I have greatly enjoyed taking my church family on these joy journeys and watching them grow in Christ. Every year they look forward to my holiday greeting that includes a schedule of coming sermon scriptures and titles during the Advent season through the first Sunday of the new year. Examples of the holiday letter and Advent/Christmas schedule can be found in Appendices C and D.

As the congregation grows, I must continue to find ways to share and express my love and the joy that I possess.

A Theological Examination of the Psalmist Model

Because it is my express intent and desire to have a joyful church, I study and preach a lot from the Book of Psalms. Walter Brueggemann's introductory comments in his book, *The Message of the Psalms: A Theological Commentary,* indicate that "the Book of Psalms provides the most reliable theological, pastoral, and liturgical resource given in the biblical tradition" (1984, 15). As Brueggemann notes, generation after generation, faithful women and men turn to the Psalms as a most helpful resource for spiritual communion with God in the daily mundane struggles of life (1984, 15). The Psalms meet deep needs, and also take us to high heights.

David, King of Israel, the poet of many of the Psalms helps us to understand both sides of joy. There are *Psalms of Orientation, Psalms of Disorientation, and Psalms of New Orientation.* Brueggemann describes these phases of life as follows:

- **Psalms of Orientation** articulate the joy, delight, goodness, coherence, and reliability of God, God's creation, and God's governing law. "Human life consists in satisfied seasons of well-being that evokes gratitude for the constancy of blessing" (Brueggemann 1984, 19).

- **Psalms of Disorientation** articulate lament in a disarray of painful experiences. "Human life consists in anguished seasons of hurt, alienation, suffering, and death. These evoke rage, resentment, self-pity, and hatred" (Brueggemann 1984, 19).

- **Psalms of New Orientation** speak boldly about a new gift from God, a fresh intrusion that makes all things new. "Human life consists in turns of surprise when we are overwhelmed with the new gifts of God, when joy breaks through despair. Where there has been only darkness, there is light" (Brueggemann 1984, 19).

Brueggemann suggests that there are two moves of faith in the Psalms: the move we make out of a settled orientation into a season of disorientation and a move from a context of disorientation to a new orientation. The first move involves the dismantling of the old when one becomes aware of a changed circumstance. A period of rage, resentment, guilt, shame, isolation, despair, hatred and hostility follows this dismantling. The second move comes about just when we think all is lost and that there is no escape. Following this move to new life, comes amazement, wonder, awe, gratitude, thanksgiving and joy (Brueggemann, 1984, 20–21).

Psalms of Orientation

Brueggemann considers the Psalms of Orientation the beginning theological point for the Psalms. These Psalms express confident faith. These Psalms know God to be reliable and trustworthy. Therefore, there is a settled conclusion and doubts are removed.

Brueggemann would like us to consider five representative types of psalms that reflect this issue of well-oriented faith: Songs of Creation, Songs of Torah, Wisdom Psalms, Songs of Retribution and Occasions of Well-Being.

They are statements that describe a happy, blessed state in which the speakers are grateful for and confident in abiding, reliable gifts of life that are long-standing from time past and will endure for time to come (Brueggemann 1984, 25).

In these Psalms, life is well ordered, without chaos, the way God intended. The theological function is to praise and thank God, but there is also an important social function. Despite all the anxieties in life, these Psalms guarantee a givenness by God. This givenness is before, over and beyond us. There is a canopy of protection to which one can cling with hope that what God intended will finally triumph. This is where the Psalms move from maintenance to transformation, and the creature serves the Creator.

Psalms of Disorientation

When considering the Psalms of Disorientation, Brueggemann shares that life is not just filled with equilibrium, coherence and symmetry, but that life is also filled with disequilibrium, incoherence and unrelieved asymmetry—disorientation. The church continues to sing songs of order even when faced with situations of disorder. Our lives experience disorientation while our faith speaks orientation (Brueggemann 1984, 51). Brueggemann points out that the use of these "psalms of darkness" may appear to be acts of unfaith, but for the community that trusts God, the use of these psalms is an act of bold faith (1984, 52).

The experiences of order and disorder are all a part of life. Life is a journey through the darkness, but newness regularly comes our way without asking. Brueggemann says that the church avoids these psalms of disorientation, but life definitely cannot be managed or controlled (1984, 53). Israel did not deny the darkness, but exercised freedom of expression by embracing the darkness as a part of new life.

Brueggemann observes two factors that operate in the midst of this expression. First, the expressions are said directly to God. Secondly, in the midst of the chaos there is a God-directed order. The testimony is that *"darkness and light are both alike to thee" (Psalm 139:12).* (Brueggemann 1984, 53–54). This is a way through and out of the darkness. Brueggemann calls this an inward spiritual movement that makes a "plea to praise" movement possible (1984, 56). The prayer plea is for God to correct a situation that has become desperate. The petitioner asks God to act. The praise means that something happened. The desperate situation has turned to gratitude and joy.

Brueggemann suggests that this covenantal-theological move frees us. Whatever happens has a profound emotional, as well as theological, impact on the complainer, for a whole new world of trust and gratitude is entered into in that moment (1984, 58).

The Psalms of Disorientation could be caused by God's abandonment, Israel's infidelity or enemy hostility. Either way, there is unhappiness, but we do not have to linger there. There is the assurance of new life.

Psalms of New Orientation

Brueggemann has shown a major move from reliable order to the reality of disorientation. Disorientation is experienced and expressed in many ways. Then, the Psalmist surprises us with unexpected new life. This newness cannot be explained, but just told.

How does one explain moving from wretchedness to joy? Brueggemann explains that the question of how the move is made is a theological matter. Israel sings of new orientation because the God of Israel is the One who hears, answers and resolves disorientation. The Psalms, which are also prayers and songs, "bespeak the intervening action of God to give life in a world where death seems to have the best and strongest way" (Brueggemann 1984, 125). God causes new life when others suggest none is even possible.

One obvious song of new orientation is one of thanksgiving. Psalm 30 sings of *"going into trouble and coming out again"* (Brueggemann 1984, 126). The psalmist was healed, lifted up and restored. The end results are praise and thanksgiving. God gives new life, which moves one from weeping to joy; from disorientation to new orientation. It is impossible to keep silent when God gives new life. Brueggemann writes:

> The mark of new life, inexplicable and unexpected, is confession expressed as thanks. Such thanks, which articulates a new life commitment, is possible only among those who vividly remember their prerescue situation (1984, 127–128).

God wants something from newly rescued people. God wants new obedience, new songs, new embracing and new delights. The writer of Psalm 40 tells the glad news, speaking of God's faithfulness without holding back words. The writer of Psalm 34 remembers his moment of rescue. He also gives instructions on how to sustain this new orientation and counsels others with his wisdom. Walter Brueggemann writes, "the newly oriented Israel must engage in society building, to develop forms of behavior, which sustain the gift of new social possibility" (1984, 133).

The Book of Psalms is a source of comfort and joy for every day the Lord gives. The Psalms soothe the soul in every season: seasons of peace, pain and when everything becomes brand new. *"Weeping may linger for the night, but joy comes with the morning" (Psalm 30:5)*

The Psalmist Model of Spiritual Joy truly embraces the Psalms. In 2004, I preached twenty-one sermons on Psalm 91. Why? To reinforce that God cares, loves, rescues and protects His people. God wants us to share with the world the reason why we can sing for joy, even when we are IN trouble.

Chapter Six

The Joy of the Journey

When I look back on my growth into pastoral ministry, I now see that there were five years of "giving away my joy" that defined how I serve my congregation. During those five years, I focused on building a healthy marriage between pastor and people. Each year, I focused on a different aspect of that relationship to grow my people into a joy-filled congregation that is willing to share their joy with others. It has been a joyous journey. My years of service have brought me great joy.

My pastorate began in March 1999. Every year, I celebrate our anniversary by choosing a theme that reflects the hearts of my people. Each year, I write a message to my flock that shares my reflections on the past year and my hope for our future. The following briefly describes my focus during the first five years that shaped my ministry and includes my anniversary messages to my flock, "Words From Pastor J."

My First Year (March 1999–March 2000)

When my pastorate began in March 1999, New Prospect had been without a pastor for two and a half years. My focus during the first year was to restore their hope by planting the gospel in their hearts.

The theme for the first anniversary of the marriage between pastor and people was "Celebrating the Presence of a Pastor." It was based on Jeremiah 3:15, *"I will give you shepherds after my own heart, who will feed you with knowledge and understanding."*

Words From Pastor J

Bless the wonderful name of Jesus! I have loved the New Prospect Missionary Baptist Church family all my life. I just didn't know who they were. But now that I know them and love them, I will continue to hold them and try my best to never let them go. For 24 years, 5 months and 14 days, the Lord molded and shaped me to pastor New Prospect Missionary Baptist Church. When Reverend Russell Fox, Sr., the late Reverend Dr. E. A. Freeman and the Reverend Dr. Charles G. Adams ministered to me, God knew what He was doing. I kneel in awe and give God much thanks. For a year, pastor and people have been a blessing to each other. Hallelujah to Jesus!

We are still celebrating the tremendous opportunity we have as a church. We have the Word, the treasures to equip and fill the hearts of God's people with blessed hope. We have a God, and we have a Savior. Together, in the name of Jesus, we can create a family of faith where we can embrace, share and live out the gospel.

The Lord keeps on revealing to me every moment of my life, that I serve a Risen Christ. I am caring for people whom God loves. They are blood-bought, and I love them. I have tried my best to teach, preach, pray, love and sing the gospel right into their hearts.

I thank my God for giving me a chance to embrace New Prospect Missionary Baptist Church. I thank God for their love, support, encouragement and prayers. I thank God for their stories that I keep in my heart. I love this family of faith!

I thank God for my husband, Dave, and my sons, Davey and Brian. They keep on loving me even when I'm not there. I feel their arms of support around me every day. I thank God for my parents and grandparents who give me a standing ovation every night. May my pastoral life fill both families with hope and truth from above.

This has been an awesome, incredible and wonderful year. Who gets the glory? GOD! Hundreds and hundreds of souls have been baptized, revived and restored. Who gets the glory? GOD! I have joy, peace and contentment doing what God has commanded. Who gets the glory? GOD!

When we wait on the Lord, the impossible becomes possible, the difficult becomes easy and the ordinary is no burden. Thank you New Prospect Missionary Baptist Church. Let us stand ready to change and touch the world with God's presence and God's power. Thank you again and again New Prospect Missionary Baptist Church!

"O holy God, my Father God, Mother God and Everything God, teach me before I teach them. Show me before I show

*them. Love me before I love them. I am Your slave. I am
Your prisoner. I am Your servant. I hear and I obey. Amen.*"

My Second Year (March 2000–March 2001)

During my second year, I focused on meeting the special
needs of special people by building our ministries. Our
anniversary theme for the second year of marriage between
pastor and people was "Celebrating the Identity of a Pastor,"
based on Galatians 2:20:

> *"I have been crucified with Christ; and it is no
> longer I who live, but it is Christ who lives in
> me. And the life I now live in the flesh I live by
> faith in the Son of God who loved me, and
> gave Himself for me."*

Words From Pastor J

We are still celebrating what God is accomplishing through
us. The vision in the hearts of this pastor and people is
glorious. We worship, we serve, and we give light and life to
others. God is so awesome! Together we have done a few
things in two years: Endowment Development, Youth
Ministry, New Prospect Missionary Baptist Church's
Scholarship Program, Outreach Fellowship, Advent and Lent
Celebrations, Substance Abuse Program, renovation of our
new administrative offices and multi-purpose rooms, the
New Prospect Missionary Baptist Church Optimist Club,
Bereavement Support Group, Radio Ministry, adoption of
Pasteur School and Power Wednesday. I give God thanks for

having His great hand upon us. Our future is even brighter as we anticipate At The Lighthouse Corporation, our computer lab and the coming church expansion projects.

I give God thanks for all the labor and so many prayers. Your commitment to spread the gospel and to grow spiritually has certainly increased. We live for God, we live for each other, and yes we live to move darkness out of this world. Remember, God is not through blessing us.

My heart is overwhelmed by the love and support from my family and friends. I can preach because I'm free. I can sing because I'm happy. In the name of Jesus, I am inspired to be something, do something and to leave something. Glory to God!

New Prospect Missionary Baptist Church, you are treasures to me and I guard you daily with my life. I love to do what I do, and I do it with my heart. I desire the people of God to grow, to become healthier, wiser and more willing servants. We are to be powerful, not popular; and it's no secret what God can do. The Word of God says:

> Come to me, all you that are weary and are carrying heavy burdens, and I will give you rest. Take my yoke upon you, and learn from me; for I am gentle and humble in heart, and you will find rest for your souls. For my yoke is easy, and my burden is light (Matthew 11:28–30).

Shine on us!

I have discovered that the greatest service I can offer to the church is prayer and the feeding of the Word of God.

Unless the Word lives in you, you cannot birth the Word in others. Thank God that I know who I am. Thank God that I know who you are, and we can't even imagine what God is about to do! Thank you again and again New Prospect Missionary Baptist Church!

My Third Year (March 2001–March 2002)

In my third year, I wanted my people to know that they were loved. I focused on loving the church into becoming a great place for the Lord. The anniversary theme for the third year of the marriage between pastor and people was "Celebrating a Pastor Called to Love." It was based on Romans 13:8, *"Owe no one anything, except to love one another; for the one who loves another has fulfilled the law."*

Words From Pastor J

God loved humanity so much that God gave Jesus to save us. That is real love. So here we are celebrating, loving and knowing that our future is alive because of real love. I place a high value on loving and caring for the people of God at New Prospect Missionary Baptist Church. It is a privilege to be called by the God of light and love; to mend the wounded, strengthen the weak and encourage those who have grown weary—just by giving some love.

As the pastor, it is my prayer that the Lord will continue to help me to motivate and communicate by loving. I can get into the hearts of those whom the Lord has placed in my care, by doing deeds of love. I have spent three years trying to grow this church stronger and deeper. We worship, fellowship, evangelize, disciple and do ministry, but not without love for one another.

I have been called to love the Lord, to love my family and to love the body of Christ. I have been called to love and to serve Jesus the Christ, who is my Savior. The greatest truth is that an Almighty God loves me. That is the message I want the people of God to embrace: that they too are loved. The late Reverend Dr. Frederick G. Sampson II, appointed me to "love like a shepherd and not rule like a general." I am grateful still for his love. Then, I think about the love the Johnson family shares day by day, in so many ways. Thank God for Dave, Davey and Brian.

New Prospect Missionary Baptist Church, I love you, and I love God! How could a Wilma "Beanie" Johnson not love the One who designed her and chose her before she was born or even knew God? I recognize my responsibility to live my own life with integrity, to faithfully communicate the Word of God, to teach, to preach, to pray and to love this congregation.

New Prospect Missionary Baptist Church, God loves you and I love you too! In the midst of our hurts and struggles, our pain and suffering, there is love. We must love one another! Love comes from God, and love casts out fear. Every day is Resurrection Day, Thanksgiving Day and "Love Me" Day.

New Prospect Missionary Baptist Church, you have a "lover" for a pastor. I want to love this church into a great place for the Lord. I love being your pastor. I have some regrets about those persons who have left because my loving them was not enough. I am only sorry that they did not stay long enough for all of us to love on. New Prospect Missionary Baptist Church, I love being your pastor. My thoughts are fixed on the Lover of my soul. Pray that I may honor you by affirming a God we can trust and a God who loves.

My Fourth Year (March 2002–March 2003)

The focus of my fourth year was to build a house of joyful people who share their joy. The theme for the fourth anniversary of marriage between pastor and people was "Celebrating a Pastor Who Gives Away Her Joy," based on the following scripture:

> *Now my head is lifted up above my enemies all around me, and I will offer in his tent sacrifices with shouts of joy; I will sing and make melody to the* LORD *(Psalm 27:6).*

Words From Pastor J

The joy of the Lord is my strength! Every single moment of my life is consecrated with the joy of the Lord. What a privilege it is to give away my joy to New Prospect Missionary Baptist Church as an offering unto my God. The gift of joy often plunges me into thanksgiving, praise and adoration for what God has done in my life. I count it all joy—my ups and downs, my victories and failures, my highs and hurts, my tragedies and triumphs—all of it, joy!

My New Prospect Missionary Baptist Church family, the Lord has empowered and encouraged this congregation in a mighty way. This is God's house of prayer, filled with many joyful people of God who share their joy. There is joy here at New Prospect Missionary Baptist Church. There is peace that passes all understanding here, and I am so grateful.

I give away my joy because of what I know. I know God is able, and I know God is a balm in Gilead. I know God gives new life. I know God is bread when we are hungry and water when we are thirsty. We have been sanctified by the precious blood of Jesus. How could we not have joy?

My New Prospect Missionary Baptist Church Family, I celebrate four years of being your pastor and the Lord's servant. You have a pastor who loves and a pastor who gives away her joy. I need your prayers as I continue to seek the Lord. I am asking for power to preach the gospel and power to follow where the Lord leads us. I am asking for undying faith as I trust God and God's promises daily.

I want to be like Jesus. I want to have an attitude like Jesus. I want to have a heart like Jesus. I want to be obedient like Jesus. Right now, I give God permission to fill me with Jesus' joy so I can give away more joy to you. Let us make a joyful noise unto our God!

My Fifth Year (March 2003–March 2004)

My focus during the fifth year was to teach my people the power of standing on the promises of God. I wanted them to know that God's Word gives us the courage and strength to continue this Christian journey regardless of the ups or downs in life.

Our anniversary theme was "Celebrating a Pastor Standing on the Promises." It was based on 2 Corinthians 7:1, *"Since we have these promises, beloved, let us cleanse ourselves from every defilement of body and spirit, making holiness perfect in the fear of God."*

Words From Pastor J

God's promises are precious. God's promises are exceedingly great gifts to the body of Christ. I am standing on the promises of God! My soul rejoices when I think about the assurance of the strength and power that God gives.

There are many promises. Some we have received and others are "not yet." But I thank God for every promise that cleanses the body and the spirit. I thank God for every promise that is new every morning.

The Word of God gives me courage and confidence. I can come out of uncertainty and not be moved by the sense of fear. I can truly stand and look the enemy in the face and declare that "I am standing on the promises of God!"

I encourage and bless all of you to have faith in God and to stand. You can stand on the promises because they are true. We can stand on the promises because they are light and life. The promises of God will paralyze the enemy. Therefore, we can march forward and wherever our feet touch down, we can stand.

The apostle Paul compares the work of the pastor to that of a soldier. This pastor/teacher needs the Word of God to fight, endure, guide, comfort and encourage. I am holding fast with all my might to the Word of God. I am standing on the promises of God.

New Prospect, thank you so very much for your thirst and hunger for the Word of God. These five years have blessed my soul as I have preached and taught the Word. Let us continue to stand together in the name of Jesus the Christ.

The Journey Continues

As I said at the beginning of this chapter, these first five years at New Prospect Missionary Baptist Church defined my ministry and the Psalmist Model of Spiritual Joy. I have just completed my sixth year (March 2004–March 2005), and the joy of the journey just keeps on coming.

This year has been especially joyous because I was diagnosed with lung cancer and half of one lung was removed. God breathed His joy on me. I can preach, and teach because every breath I take is a breath of joy. I can sing even stronger than before. God has truly placed joy bells in my soul.

The theme for our sixth anniversary of marriage between pastor and people is "Refreshed by His Presence: He Is Breathing on Me." It is based on John 20:22, *"When Jesus had said this, He breathed on them and said to them, 'Receive the Holy Spirit.'"*

Words From Pastor J

Today is March 29, 2005. I am a cancer survivor. After all I've been through, I still have joy. On November 22, 2004, I had successful lung cancer surgery. The Lord has indeed breathed mightily on me. I spent forty days out of my pulpit. I returned on New Year's Eve. Since then, every Sunday, the Lord has empowered me to teach, preach and sing about joy. So far, I have preached thirteen sermons on joy.

The world didn't give me this joy. The world can't take away this joy. Every day joy bells just keep on ringing in my soul. Every day I am refreshed by His presence and Jesus is breathing on me. With every breath that I take, I will worship the Lord!

Chapter Seven

A Review of Pastoral Leadership Literature

The literature in the field of pastoral leadership is extensive. The focus of this literature review is on materials that highlight biblical spirituality and a theology of joy.

Ministry for Social Crisis
by Dr. Forrest E. Harris, Sr.

In *Ministry for Social Crisis,* the Reverend Dr. Forrest E. Harris, Sr. states that there are four models of leadership: pastoral, prophetic, reformist and nationalistic (1993, 94). He affirms these to be the most prominent among black church leaders. Dr. Harris, who is the director of the Kelly Miller Smith Institute on the Black Church at Vanderbilt Divinity School in Nashville, Tennessee, says, "The primary objective of pastoral activity in the black church is to comfort and to console those battered by life's adverse circumstances" (1993, 94).

Dr. Harris further states, "Pastoral ministry must deal with the reality of oppression in a way that makes life more human for persons who look to their minister for care"

(1993, 95). Pastoral ministry must have love as its foundation in order to reach people where they are.

The prophetic leadership model brings the vision of social justice to life. Dr. Harris states, "When the church does not give serious theological reflection to past prophetic actions, the locus of praxis for present and future actions is lost" (1993, 98).

The emphasis of the reformist leadership model transforms an oppressive system into one that liberates. So many issues like poverty and unemployment directly affect the black community. According to Dr. Harris, "the black church should serve as a community forum for ongoing dialogue regarding the political future and social transformation of the black community" (1993, 101).

The nationalistic model of leadership is concerned with preservation of cultural identity. Its major concern is to help black people find ways to take control of their own destiny. The author shares that "while many traditional black pastors find aspects of black nationalism theologically unacceptable, one notes that many of them secretly admire the call of black nationalists for restoring dignity, self-determination, and self-respect to black people" (Harris, 1993, 102).

African American Church Growth
by Dr. Carlyle Fielding Stewart, III

The Reverend Dr. Carlyle Fielding Stewart, III is the senior pastor of Hope United Methodist Church, Southfield, Michigan. He has written a wonderful book entitled *African*

American Church Growth. Dr. Stewart had clearly reviewed all previous literature on church growth and proposed his diversity-sensitive version of church development. In other words, he synthesized the literature on church growth and outlined how African American churches could use that information.

One of the central premises of Dr. Stewart's book is his use of prophetic principles. Although he does not succinctly define prophetic principles, he does explain the concept in terms of "prophetic concern" and "prophetic ministry."

Dr. Stewart shares four basic tenets for building a prophetic pastoral/ministry leadership style: passion, conviction, investment and vision.

Passion

> Passion is the fuel which empowers the messenger to bring forth the Word of God... Those churches which exemplify passion in telling the story, preaching the Word, and reaching out to others in the larger community have been most successful in building viable congregations (Stewart 1994, 23).

Dr. Stewart has created a life center where he brings forth the Word of God with power fueled by passion. He describes prophetic passion as "the ability to sense, interpret and soulfully articulate God's Word" (1994, 23). His services are full of vitality, conviction and ardor, which are inviting, and his membership continues to increase.

Conviction

Dr. Stewart defines conviction as "the irrepressible desire or will to 'live the Word' through human experience" (1994, 27). An engine needs oil, a car needs gas and passion needs conviction. Conviction speaks of our commitment to Christ and dedication to our ministries. Dr. Stewart further states, "Conviction also involves courage, the ability to take stands that may be unpopular with parishioners, but may ultimately lead them to a new awareness of God's creative, transformative possibilities in their lives and in their communities" (1994, 29).

Dr. Stewart quotes Chogyam Trungpa, who authored *Shambhala* (New York: Bantam Books, 1986). Trungpa called pastors sacred warriors "because of the absence of fear and the presence of a confidence or conviction which makes them intrepid in owning and being what they truly are. They are motivated by an ultimate concern for the well being and wholeness of the people they serve. In essence, they are ambassadors of goodness" (Stewart 1994, 31).

Dr. Stewart calls for and encourages pastors to "stand firm and tall against the forces of evil, corruption and injustice, both inside and outside the church" (1994, 33). This conviction allows the pastor to convince others of the confidence and truth of God's Word.

Investment

Investment is described as "a desire to fully and unequivocally invest oneself in serving the Lord" (Stewart 1994, 33).

For some pastors, personal investment is a high price to pay. Jonah ran from the possibility of investing himself in Ninevah. God's personal investment for humankind involved "emptying Himself." The church must invest time and resources in those in the community. The church's availability and concern for others will achieve growth and bring people to Christ.

Vision

"Vision," Stewart states, "is a necessary part of prophetic ministry, for the pastor as prophet must have an eye for the future, taking people and moving them toward the higher reality" (1994, 35). Dr. Stewart shares that Moses' ministry involved the movement of people's minds, hearts and spirits as well as their physical bodies. All of the prophets had vision. Stewart quotes Edgar Magnin as saying "Isaiah envisioned the day when the lion would be turned into plowshares...when every man would dwell under his own vine and fig tree and none would be afraid" (Stewart 1994, 36).

Prophetic vision is critical to the African-American church. In the American dream, the cry for "liberty and justice for all" is based upon a vision. The African-American church has always had hope and faith that "God can and God will prevail in the context of human community" (Stewart 1994, 36). Dr. Stewart also made the following observation:

> For African American people, the church is still the most vitally progressive force in the life of

their communities. If the church remains silent in the midst of the evils of injustice, how will the people have a voice to adjudicate their concerns?...Whenever a church speaks out with righteous indignation its stature often rises in the eyes of the community (1994, 37).

A prophetic pastor must have visions of more than "a new heaven and a new earth." Prophetic pastors must have ministry styles that make visions a reality. There is a future and preparing for the future in the present means one has possessed the vision. "The ability to anticipate, expect, envision and implement visions from God is a critical component of prophetic ministry and a useful aid in promoting the church's potential" (Stewart 1994, 38).

When the Multitude Comes
by Dr. Sam Davis

The Reverend Dr. Sam Davis is the senior pastor of Beulah Grove Baptist Church in Augusta, Georgia. He feels that the concept of values should not be overlooked in the pastoral/ministry styles of a leader. In his book, *When The Multitude Comes,* Dr. Davis tells how Beulah Grove Baptist Church adopted the following values (2001, 52):

- Embrace and operate, at all times, on the spiritual principles taught by Jesus Christ and outlined in the Bible.
- Create a diverse, inclusive environment aimed at serving all souls from the cradle to the grave.

- Train persons in church leadership at all levels in order to ensure that the direction provided to their divisions and ministries is aligned with the values, mission and goals of the church.

- Create and maintain a plan of education for its members and the community to ensure a consistent understanding of the vision mission and outcome goals of the church.

The Battle Is the Lord's
by Dr. Benjamin Stanley Baker

The Reverend Dr. Benjamin Stanley Baker is the Senior Pastor of the New Light Baptist Church located in Detroit, Michigan. In his book, *The Battle Is the Lord's*, he shares seven pastoral leadership styles:

1. **Shepherd:** A pastor-shepherd must see, serve and be sensitive to God's sheep. "Once you see them and come to them, you must seek for sensitivity as to where they are, why they are where they are, and what needs to be done to get them where they need to go" (Baker 2002, 82). Pastors must lead the sheep to the Good Shepherd who supplies all of our needs.

2. **Overseer:** A pastor-overseer must oversee by feeding, training, leading and caring for the sheep. "The pastor-overseer must be 'over' his people in the sense that he is aware and knowledgeable of this people" (Baker 2002, 85). The pastor-overseer knows the needs of the sheep and in turn gives them what they

need to survive and mature. The sheep must grow in possessing the fruit of the spirit. Baker states, "The pastor-overseer must not narrow his perspective down merely to seeing certain areas in the life of the church or dealing with certain departments or auxiliaries. The pastor as overseer has the divinely appointed responsibility of overseeing the whole flock" (Baker 2002, 84).

3. **Supervisor:** A pastor-supervisor must understand the function, mission and purposes of the church in order to supervise. "The purpose and function of the church are evangelism, education and edification. The evangelistic thrust of the church is to reach, teach, win and develop persons for Jesus Christ." Baker says that the "second function of the church is Christian education" where "the church has the responsibility, in conjunction with the family to teach Christian ideals, practices and ethics." His third function, edification, focuses on building, restoring and lifting up the people to make them stronger (Baker 2002, 87). The pastor-supervisor helps the sheep reach their greatest potential by guiding, directing and demonstrating ministry.

4. **Organizer:** A pastor-organizer directs the church to be Christ-centered. Faithful volunteers are needed to serve in Christ-centered ministries. The church must do what Christ commands. "The objective of the pastor-organizer is to organize, arrange, set in order

and fix action programs for specific purposes and use selected procedures to accomplish the pastoral task" (Baker 2002, 92).

5. **Enabler:** A pastor-enabler realizes that one person cannot do all the work and therefore he involves his members based on the talents and gifts that God has given to them. The Holy Spirit has equipped and empowered every Christian to work and serve. The pastor-enabler must understand that the Holy Spirit is working through every believer to get the job done. "Spiritual gifts have a two-fold purpose: to strengthen the church's fellowship and extend the church's witness and ministry" (Baker 2002, 97).

6. **Administrator:** Dr. Baker defines administration as "the task of discovering and clarifying the goals and purpose of the field it serves and of moving in a coherent, comprehensive manner toward their realization" (2002, 106). Pastor-administrators move the church to discover their goals and clarify their purpose. Once the goals and objectives have been clarified, they "move to the second step of defining what means will help in reaching the desired goal" (Baker 2002, 107). Pastor-administrators know where they are trying to go, and they put into action ways to reach their destiny. The pastor-administrator must concentrate on resources and leadership possibilities and share them with the church. Dr. Baker suggests that pastor-administrators should see themselves

"as the conductor of an orchestra wanting the very best sound" (2002, 108). The process steps of recognizing the need, planning, organizing, staffing, directing, coordinating, communicating, and budgeting should help establish an effective administration (Baker 2002, 109–111).

7. **Counselor:** "The goal of spiritual counseling is to bring men and women into right relationship with God and to lead them into the abundant life" (Baker 2002, 113). The task of the pastor-counselor is to "comfort those who are troubled; give guidance to the perplexed; bring 'deliverance to the captives'; give assurance of forgiveness to the penitent; give courage to the sick and bereaved; and to meet the personal needs of the members who comprise the congregation" (Baker 2002, 114). These things are done by listening and totally depending upon Jesus.

Surprising Insights From the Unchurched
by Thom S. Rainer

In his book, *Surprising Insights From the Unchurched,* Thom S. Rainer writes about the following ten leadership styles for the leaders of churches to use in assessing themselves and their effectiveness in reaching the un-churched (2001, 181–182):

- **Delegator oriented:** Leads by assigning tasks in nearly every situation

- **Dream oriented:** Spends a lot of time dreaming big dreams with little concern for completion
- **Goal oriented:** Sets goals and pushes for completion
- **Knowledge oriented:** Leads by superior knowledge and understanding rather than by example
- **Loner oriented:** Prefers to work alone and risks accomplishing little
- **Organization oriented:** Is organized above all else, and checks every detail
- **Relationship oriented:** Highly interested in people, feelings and fellowship
- **Suggestion oriented:** Leads by making suggestions to others
- **Task oriented:** Interested in production and getting things done
- **Team player oriented:** Must work in a group or be a part of a team effort; leads primarily by example

When God Builds a Church
by Bob Russell

In his book, *When God Builds a Church,* Bob Russell observed, after talking to people and visiting churches, that there is a desperate need for good leadership in most churches. "There is a leadership void in our churches. Russell states, "There is a hunger for dedicated, charismatic personalities who can inspire others to follow" (2000, 74). He believes the reason God has blessed the Southeast Christian Church, where he pastors, is excellent leadership.

Pastor Russell also believes that God is looking for consecrated, committed church leaders. Leaders should be more concerned with who they are and not so much with what they do. Integrity, trustworthiness, sincerity and effort, demonstrated by people who want to live like Jesus Christ, are necessary for church growth. Pastor Russell says:

> A lack of integrity among the leaders quenches the flow of the Holy Spirit and removes God's hand of blessing from the church...For God's hand of blessing to be upon your church, there must be a degree of holiness among the leaders. God doesn't require perfection, but He does require sincerity and effort...If you are not living a life of purity either God's Spirit will not bless your congregation, or He will move you out of the way (2000, 75–77).

Escape From Church, Inc.
by E. Glenn Wagner

In *Escape From Church, Inc.* (Grand Rapids, MI: Zondervan, 1999), E. Glenn Wagner speaks to the need for pastoral theology and makes a distinction between "leadership" and "shepherdship." Wagner writes that pastoral theology, as defined by Seward Hiltner, is:

> ...a formal branch of theology resulting from study of Christian shepherding...It is that branch or field of theological knowledge and inquiry that brings the shepherding perspective to bear upon all the operations and functions of the church and the minister.

Shepherding is in some degree present in everything done by pastor or church (1999, 69–70).

Wagner asks, "What happens when 'leadership' rather than 'shepherdship' becomes the primary model for the pastor?" (1999, 142) He then compares the two and suggests these differences: Leaders look at people as products and objects. They manage, only seeking church growth, focusing on programs and seeking self-fulfillment. They guide by a business model. Shepherds, however, make people a priority. They encourage, minister, know people and call them by name. They guide by a biblical model and seek spiritual fullness. Wagner believes that "a leader model can never produce the kind of church that will transform the culture around it. Only a shepherd model can do that." He attests that is why God does not call us to be leaders, but shepherds. "If our goal is faithful shepherdship, the result will be effective leadership" (Wagner 1999, 142).

King David is known today not so much as a leader, but as a shepherd-king.

He chose David his servant and took him from the sheep pens; from tending the sheep he brought him to be the shepherd of his people Jacob, of Israel his inheritance. And David shepherded them with integrity of heart; with skillful hands he led them (Psalm 78:70–72 NIV).

Wagner says, "a pastor who thinks of himself as a leader more than a shepherd will tend to give priority to projects over people and chores over community" (1999, 144).

In a discussion of the place of vision to leadership, Wagner says that though vision is wonderful and a necessary component to leadership, the flock needs to see a shepherd's heart first. "My first responsibility as pastor is to build my credibility as a faithful shepherd, not to convince people to buy into my vision for the church" (Wagner 1999, 147). Vision grows out of earned trust. "That means the number one goal for a pastor is not to articulate a great vision but to help his sheep trust him and know him" (Wagner 1999, 148).

Leadership for a Changing Church
by Robert Dale

In his book, *Leadership for a Changing Church,* Robert Dale suggests that there are two angles for leadership: mission and morale. He says, "Mission, variously called vision, tasks, goals, direction, dreams, external outcomes, market niches, calling, congregational personality—answers the basic question: What will we do?" (Dale 1998, 67) However, he continues, "Morale, sometimes referred to as *esprit de corps,* the spirit of the group, fellowship, internal care, congregational well being—makes the basic affirmation, 'We can do it!'" (1998, 68) Mission takes skill, stability, tradition, commitment and action. Morale takes will, loyalty, trust, confidence and attitude (Dale 1998, 69). But Dale insists that effective leadership involves both mission and morale, and that leaders are "responsible for assuring balanced or blended emphasis on mission and morale within the organization" (1998, 67).

Nine Marks of a Healthy Church
by Mark Dever

Mark Dever, senior pastor of Capitol Hill Baptist Church in Washington, D.C., challenges pastors to take their responsibilities to the local church seriously. In *Nine Marks of a Healthy Church,* he gives a powerful call for imperfect churches to be healthy. He focuses on "two basic needs in our churches: the preaching of the message and the leading of disciples" (Dever 2000, 14). The first need covers five of the nine marks:

- Expositional preaching
- Biblical theology
- A biblical understanding of the Gospel
- A biblical understanding of conversion
- A biblical understanding of evangelism

The second need covers the last four marks:

- A biblical understanding of church membership
- A biblical understanding of church discipline;
- A concern for discipleship and growth
- Biblical church leadership (Dever 2000, 15–17).

Pastor Dever states that the first mark of a healthy church, and the main role of any pastor, is expositional preaching (2000, 25). Expositional preaching begins with a topic. The topic is constructed around various texts and stories, and a particular theme is developed. The Word of God is unfolded and given to the people because the pastor has been challenged by the Word to preach. The people deserve to hear and know God's words. Pastor Dever suggests that the most important thing to look for in a church is the preaching of the Word. Paul told Timothy in 2 Timothy 4:2 (NIV), *"Preach the Word."* Why this priority? Pastor Dever says, "Because this Word is the word of life (Philippians 2:16). That is the great task of the preacher: to hold out the word of life to people who need it for their souls" (2000, 39).

Not only must pastors preach the Word of God, but their sermons must also teach about the nature and character of God, which is the second mark of a healthy church. Pastor Dever summarizes that the Bible teaches us five important things about God. The fact is that God is creating (Dever 2000, 46). God created the world, and He created people. Secondly, God is holy, and we are guilty and separated from God. Churches need to tell people how to find forgiveness for their sins and how to find new life (Dever 2000, 52). Thirdly, God is faithful, and He is faithful to His promises. God promised a Messiah who came, was punished for our guilt and restored our relationship with God. Fourthly, God is loving. He has a special love for His people. As John wrote:

> *"This is love: not that we loved God, but that He loved us and sent His Son as an atoning sacrifice for our sins...We love because He first loved us"* (1 John 4:10, 19 NIV).

Finally, God is also sovereign.

> If we are to be a healthy church in such times, we must be especially careful to pray for leaders in the church to have a biblical grasp of and an experiential trust in the sovereignty of God (Dever 2000, 59).

The third mark of a healthy church is that there is good news in the Bible. Dever states, "Christianity is all about news" (2000, 65). He continues:

> True Christianity is realistic about the dark side of our world, our life, our nature, our heart. But true Christianity is not finally pessimistic or morally indifferent, encouraging us merely to just settle in and accept the truth about our fallen state (Dever 2000, 69).

At the same time, Pastor Dever suggests that the gospel message of "Good news is not simply that God is love" (2000, 70). It is not simply that Jesus wants to be our Friend. It is not simply that we should live right. The good news is that God has plans for us. There is good news in the Bible that teaches us to live with a growing faith and a certain hope. It is good news that God is love, spirit and holy.

Dever shares that the good news of Christianity has a specific cognitive content (2000, 78). "To really hear the gospel," he says, "is to be shaken to your core. To really hear the gospel is to change" (2000, 81). It is to have a personal relationship with God.

The fourth mark of a healthy church is conversion. Pastor Dever suggests we ask five questions to get a biblical understanding of conversion:

- Is change needed? (2000, 84)
- Is change really possible? (2000, 87)
- What change is needed? (2000, 88)
- What will this change involve? (2000, 89)
- How does this great change happen? (2000, p.92)

People have a deep longing for change. The Bible speaks about the state of our human nature as being in debt, slavery, bankrupt and/or dead (Dever 2000, 87). A change is needed for our condition, and change is possible. We need to repent, and turn from sin and to God. Dever states:

> The real change that we need is this conversion from worshipping ourselves to worshipping God, from being guilty in ourselves before God to being forgiven in Christ (2000, 89).

Pastor Dever also says, "The change that we need is a change from living guilt-incurring lives of sin, to living forgiven lives of trust in Christ" (2000, 100). This type of change comes only by God's grace.

The fifth mark of a healthy church is evangelism. Dever suggests the following questions be considered to understand and practice evangelism:

- Who should evangelize?
- How should we evangelize?
- What is evangelism?
- Why should we evangelize? (2000, 106)

We find evangelism throughout the New Testament. Not just Paul and the apostles, but all of Jesus' disciples evangelized. All Christians should spread the good news in order to reach people with the gospel. We want to tell the truth about God and about Jesus Christ because our telling brings joy. Pastor Dever gives six biblical guidelines on how to evangelize:

- Be honest about repentance. It is costly (2000, 112).
- Tell people there is an urgency of the message. If they repent and believe, they will be saved, but they must do it now (2000, 113).
- Tell people with joy to repent and, however difficult it may be, it is worth a relationship with God. A relationship with forgiveness, purpose and hope is worth it (2000, 115).
- Use the Bible. Learn it so you can share it with others (2000, 115).
- Realize that the lives of individuals and the church as a whole should give credibility to what we proclaim (2000, 115).
- Remember the importance of prayer, "because salvation is the work of God" (2000, 116).

The sixth mark of a healthy church is church membership. Pastor Dever dealt with the questions:

- What is the definition of a church?
- Why should one join a church?
- What is entailed in church membership?

> According to the New Testament, the church is primarily a body of people who profess and give evidence that they have been saved by God's grace alone, for His glory alone, through faith alone, in Christ alone (Dever 2000, 135).

Joining a church gives the assurance that we belong to each other and are known by one another. We join a church to connect with others in spreading the gospel at home and abroad (Dever 2000, 139). We join a church to make the truth known that it is God's love in Christ that saves us. We join a church to help build up other believers (Dever 2000, 140). They see a life that Christ changed because of a relationship with Him. Dever states:

> Church membership is our opportunity to grasp hold of each other in responsibility and love. By identifying ourselves with a particular church, we let pastors and other members of that local church know that we intend to be committed in attendance, giving, prayer and service (Dever 2000, 143).

Pastor Dever also says "joining a church increases our sense of ownership of the work of the church, of its community, of its budget, of its goals" (2000, 143).

The seventh mark of a healthy church is church discipline. Unfortunately, when we hear the term *church discipline,* we tend to think only of the negative aspects, such as correction (Dever 2000, 155). However, there are many Bible scriptures concerning church discipline. In Hebrews 12, church discipline is presented as a positive thing, and

God disciplines (Dever 2000, 159). In addition, there are many references to church discipline in the epistles of Paul. Despite how strong or severe some of them may be, he reminds us not to practice church discipline for revenge. We should correct only out of love.

> Biblical church discipline is simple obedience to God and a simple confession that we need help...Our purpose in church discipline is positive for the individual disciplined, for other Christians as they see the real danger of sin, for the health of the church as a whole, and for the corporate witness of the church to those outside (Dever 2000, 178).

The eighth mark of a healthy church is a concern for discipleship and growth. Dever writes, "A healthy church is characterized by a serious concern for spiritual growth on the part of its members. In a healthy church, people want to get better at following Jesus Christ" (2000, 184). We should help each other grow by working, praying, giving, learning and walking together. Spiritual growth is vital. It is a sign that the church is alive. It is a biblical concept that seems to have existed from creation (Dever 2000, 191).

The ninth mark of a healthy church is leadership. Dever's prayer is that God would provide good leaders with spiritual gifts and pastoral concern. Pastor Dever asserts:

> Instead of searching for leaders with secular qualifications, we are to search for people of character, reputation, ability to handle the Word, and who display the fruit of the Spirit in their lives. Those are the kinds of people we

should recognize and into whose hands we should commit the responsibility of leading a congregation (2000, 218).

There must be a recognition and respect for godly authority in the church. Dever cites the writings of Eugene Kennedy and Sara Charles who suggest that healthy authority matches the needs and goals of serious intimate relationships because its concern is not to overcome others, but to fuel the growth of people who feel safe with each other (Williams and Williams 2000, 228). When we exercise authority the right way we display God's image to His creation (Dever 2000, 228).

Love is the foundation of the Psalmist Model of Spiritual Joy. For that reason, it reaches the young and the old. I believe the Word of God is preached with passion, power and conviction at New Prospect. The vision for the church has a past and a future that the people can see. They see their pastor investing her time, talents and treasures, and it motivates them to do the same. The psalmist model of leads and shepherds, shepherds and leads. It is a challenge and a blessing to grow a healthy church that disciples, evangelizes, educates, pampers and cares for its flock.

Chapter Eight

Evidence That Joy Works

On a Sunday in January 2003, members and visitors attending worship services at New Prospect Missionary Baptist Church received a Joy Survey from the Usher Ministry, who distributed and collected them for my review. I made a plea from the pulpit to the congregants of both worship services at 7:30 a.m. and 11:00 a.m. Seven hundred and forty-nine people took the time to stay after service to complete the survey. The sermon I preached on that Sunday was "You Ain't Seen Nothing Yet!"

The ages of those who participated in this ministry event ranged from 12–72 and above. The majority of respondents were members of New Prospect Missionary Baptist Church and female. Specific information concerning the gender and age of the participants may be found in Appendix F.

The respondents were asked to report how many worship services they attended a month. Eighty percent of the respondents attended church on a regular basis. Specific information concerning worship service attendance may be found in Appendix G.

The respondents were asked what attracted them most to attend worship services at New Prospect Missionary Baptist Church. Out of the five possible answers, the most important reason given was the preaching/teaching. Ninety-five percent of the females and eighty-four percent of the males attended for the preaching/teaching. Specific information concerning the reasons for attendance may be found in Appendix H.

The respondents were asked what they value most in a pastor. Out of the sixteen possible answers, both males and females valued the Word of God and preaching/teaching skills. Specific information regarding what the respondents valued most may be found in Appendix I.

On Sunday, November 30, 2003, an announcement was made from the pulpit at both worship services, asking those who had completed the Joy Survey in January to write their names and phone numbers on paper that I provided. I made absolutely sure that each name was on a separate slip of paper that was the same color and size. My staff assisted me in folding the papers exactly the same way and placing them in a container.

My staff members then randomly selected thirteen names. There were twelve females and one male. Seven were age 50 or above. Five were between the ages 18–35. One was between the ages 36–50. Four were members of the church and had joined prior to March 1, 1999, when I became the pastor. One had held membership at New Prospect Missionary Baptist Church from 1987 to 1996 and later returned to the church in 1999. Eight had joined under my leadership. Each person was personally contacted by my secretary and asked to meet with me on December 9, 2003 to participate in a Ministry Joy Questionnaire.

Also, on November 30, 2003, I personally selected thirteen persons to complete the Ministry Joy Questionnaire. I asked the Holy Spirit to help me choose a diverse group. There were eight females and five males. Eight were 50 or above. Two were between the ages 36–50. Three were between the ages 18–35. Seven were members of the church who had joined prior to March 1, 1999, when I became the pastor. Six joined under my leadership. My secretary personally contacted each of them and they were asked to meet with me on December 10, 2003.

Examples of the Ministry Joy Survey and Ministry Joy Questionnaire are in Appendices E and J, respectively.

Ministry Joy Survey Results

I was pleased and not surprised with the responses to the twelve survey questions. Seven hundred forty-nine people completed the survey. Three fourths of the respondents were female. Fifty percent of the female respondents were between 42–71 years of age. Most of the men who responded were between the ages of 27–71. Eighty percent of the respondents attend church on a regular basis.

The most important reasons respondents attended worship services was for the preaching, fellowship and music. The Word of God and preaching skills were the two most valued things the female respondents looked for in a pastor. Compassion, honesty and leadership were valued next by the females. The Word of God and preaching skills were the two most valued things the male respondents looked for in a pastor. Honesty, prayer life, and leadership were valued next by the males.

Many of the answers to some of the questions were similar. Following is a representative sample of responses to the questions: How does my joy that I give away through music and praise lift your spirits? Does this psalmist ministry style of giving away my joy help you give away your joy? (See complete survey in Appendix E.)

Males Ages 12–26

- "Because I see you helping so many, I want to do it too. I learned from you that God gives me all the help and support I need. Whenever I am down, your joy seems to rub off on me and my spirit is lifted."

- "The way you explain things is very clear to the point where I feel much better about myself and others. It's fulfilling to hear the music and prayers. It is uplifting to be able to understand. When you speak on the difficult tasks before us, you remind us to be strong in spirit and not crumble under pressure and to trust in the Lord and we will prosper."

- "You help me give joy by loving others. I know God has provided my life with joy through the Word. You lift my spirits the way you teach the Word."

- "I try to get my friends to come to church. My week gets started with happiness and God continues to bless me. Your personal one-on-one relationship with us helps me. Your concern for me as a person helps me. You are down to earth."

- "The individual and shared appreciation of the Word of God and the love for your sheep helps and motivates me to continue to share my joy and blessing with others. The emphasis on unity through fellowship and the joyful word on every Sunday with a sense of humor and sensitive caring personality gives me joy. Your love for God and His sheep and your positive influence lifts my spirit."

Females Ages 12–26

- "I am inspired to love with the love of Christ. I carry your messages all week and all month and all year."

- "You inspire me to help others. I understand the Word of God, and I am better acquainted with God. You make me feel the Word in my soul."

- "You teach me how to share things instead of keeping them to myself. My family has become closer together. Your music touches my heart."

- "I am learning how to be more giving. I have become a faithful tither, and I continue to look to God when confused."

- "I go out and witness and spread what I get from your services. I have grown spiritually and that has added joy. You are contagious."

Males Ages 27–41

- "Your joy helps me share my experience with others to share my joy and give it away to others. The church is filled with the Spirit. You are an anointed teacher."

- "I have learned to be a light in people's lives, and I don't have to dwell on the mistakes of my past. Your music and praise are gifts from God, and you don't keep them to yourself. I come to church, and I am taught the Word of God."

- "Through your ministry, I have learned to give away my joy. I now know about spiritual blessings that money can't buy. Your song preparation is always spiritually uplifting. I have a chance to spread the Word to others. I know that I can share my love and blessings with others."

- "Your contagious, selfless example inspires me to do the same acts for my walk in life. You feed my family with wisdom, guidance and direction. Your music and praise is beyond belief, and you have been a blessing to me and my family."

- "I find myself inviting folks who need joy to church. God has replaced my secular family with my church family. I like the way you tie the sermon and song together."

Females Ages 27–41

- "Your joy is contagious. Your joy is released when you speak, sing and teach. Your joy is a comfort through the anointing of the Holy Spirit. You make me want to help others. You lift my spirits, and I am encouraged to come more often."

- "I now spread joy to my family and friends. I get a new outlook and perspective on life each and every Sunday I leave. You give me something to believe in and to look forward to, and it's a wonderful feeling."

- "Your passion for God's Word is obvious and thus serves as an example to share my joy and passion with others. Your songs, at the end of your sermons, are always appropriate and sometimes summarize your sermons. Your music lifts my spirits. I leave church with those melodies lifting my spirit."

- "You uplift me and fill me so that I want to share with others. I have a hunger to learn more. I spiritually grow and I have learned to forgive myself. You comfort and nurture. Don't stop singing!"

- "I have learned from you that it is selfish to not share your joy. I am encouraged by your teachings to love others as God loves me. I leave each service inspired and with hope."

Males Ages 42–56

- "I constantly share with others about the Lord and His Word. You lift my spirits through the Word and the songs and they carry me through the week. Something is always said that is appropriate to what I'm going through."

- "I see an example of being a servant in you. I am interested in devoting myself to prayer and service now. You motivate encouragement and service."

- "I desire to bring joy to others and to spread the Word. You let me know of the rewards and grace to come."

- "You help me maintain joy with my disability. I feel good."

- "Your unselfish attitude inspires me. I attend services, and I see the light of day. I am mentally and physically uplifted here. The Word lifts my spirits."

Females Ages 42–56

- "Your style, and your love of Christ resonate in the church."

- "It gives me a sense of closeness to God, and I truly can feel blessed that I can continue to receive His love."

- "It reinforces to me just how good God is. I learn through your music and your praise, and it warms my heart."

- "It motivates me; it strengthens me, and encourages me to also give joy to others."
- "I feel the Spirit of God in you and you have a way of passing that Spirit to me. Because of that, I carry the Spirit of God in me always."

Males Ages 57–71

- "It often lifts burdens and sorrows."
- "When I see your joy and the way you share, it lifts me."
- "It gives me hope."
- "It makes me thank God that I am alive."
- "It helped me to see the good works of the Holy Spirit."

Females Ages 57–71

- "It makes me more compassionate and forgiving."
- "In every way my spirits are lifted, and I feel like I can face the next storm in my life easier."
- "It shows me God's great joy through song. You are truly a blessing and inspiration to me."
- "I may feel down from my personal life before I hear the message, but I am filled with new hope afterwards."
- "It calms and soothes my heart and uplifts me and inspires me. It encourages and gives me peace."

Male Ages 72 and over

- "I am more loving."
- "I want to help others."
- "I feel better about myself."
- "You give me joy every time I see you and I want to give joy."

Females Ages 72 and Over

- "You explain in a way all ages can understand."
- "I now want to tell about the love of God."
- "You give of yourself each day and I want to give of myself."
- "I am more giving now because I can hear and feel God's Spirit."
- "I feel like giving more of my time to help, love and encourage others."

Ministry Joy Questionnaire Results

I was pleased with the details given in response to all the questions. As a leader, I was encouraged to learn that so many of my congregants have a deep understanding of theological joy and the meaning of doing ministry.

One of my young adults responded to the question about the reasons for church growth at New Prospect Missionary Baptist Church by saying:

> I personally believe New Prospect Missionary Baptist Church has grown due to the new leadership of our Pastor. She makes people feel

welcomed. She also has a way of preaching, teaching to the congregation that opens at least my eyes to things in my life; helping me to take what I have learned through her teaching and my readings and applying it to my life everyday. And I believe this to be true for many other members. Not to mention the love and joy that shines from the pulpit.

Another participant who is over fifty and has been a member since 1983 answered the church growth question as follows:

Pastor Johnson's ability to make a stranger welcome is something to behold. She reaches out to others that are not members of New Prospect Missionary Baptist Church. News travels, and everyone wants to be somebody. Pastor Johnson is blessed with a charismatic personality.

Many of the answers were similar, yet revealing and different.

Below are the selected group's responses to the question: Has the theme of theological joy, as demonstrated by this pastor, impacted your ministry as a Christian?

- "It has made me want to give more, share more, do more and to help others find this joy of giving and receiving."

- "Because I believe that I am sitting under Pastor J by divine appointment, I am studying her style of leadership so that I can learn and reap from her examples in teaching so that I might do and be better in my own ministry. I know and see that joy allows you to patiently wait on God—with praise and thanksgiving, at whatever stage or place you may be. I think that is an underlying theme in much of what Pastor J shares, and I have been enriched by it.

- "Pastor J. demonstrates a God-given joy, the only kind God can give. She has never allowed any one or any situation to destroy what God has given her. I have learned to keep that kind of joy in my heart."

- "Outside of my church, I do more for people, helping them to see the Lord."

- "Absolutely! I am able to know joy through the Word of God and recognize the distractions that are not of God's Kingdom. I am also able to share that joy through what I do and how I live. I am sharing those blessings and teachings with others."

Following are the random group's responses to the question: What are the reasons for church growth at New Prospect Missionary Baptist Church?

- "Church growth at New Prospect Missionary Baptist Church is a result of the Lord sending us a magnificent pastor/teacher. Sometimes she preaches on topics that truly hit home, but because we know that she loves us we accept whatever it is."

- "I believe the reason for church growth at New Prospect Missionary Baptist Church is Pastor Johnson's obedience to God. The second reason is because of a very strong prayer life and the influence on the congregation to pray for not just the believers, but the unbelievers; and finally having faith in God, believing He will do just what He said He will do."

- "One to one contact with members. The ability to have prayer, study time and time to have spiritual fun with other Christians."

- "Church growth at New Prospect Missionary Baptist Church is so great because of the love that comes from the leader, her teaching ministry (Bible verses to back-up teachings), compassionate members, a friendly atmosphere, willingness to give to members as well as non-members and a very big giving spirit."

- "I feel strong Bible study, a strong Sunday School and a strong pastor are reasons for church growth. Without Bible study or Sunday School you really don't know why you're following the Lord or even if you want to. But I really feel a church is only going to go as far as the pastor goes. If the pastor is weak the church will struggle. If the pastor is strong the church will go far."

When the respondents were asked to describe New Prospect Missionary Baptist Church in the past, some of the selected group members responded as follows:

- "Dead!"

- "For the 7:30 a.m. worship service only 125 members, 11:00 a.m. worship service, 75. No smiling faces."

- "We were not growing. Our membership was down. We were at a stand still."

- "There was love for the Lord, but I don't believe there was love for each other."

Some of the participants from the random group responded with the following comments:

- "The Word of God has always gone forth from the pulpit."
- "No unity between the pastor and the staff."
- "Although I cannot say it felt cold in the church, I don't remember the sense of warmth as I do now."

Of the twenty-six participants, twenty-five responded to the question, "Have you personally been changed by my Pastoral Leadership?" by saying that their lives and their thinking had changed.

Chapter Nine

Reflections

I have a desire to serve. It is like fire inside of my heart and my bones. It is a joy to serve the people of God. When I reflect on the fact that Jesus served me with His very life, I must serve.

The authors of *Leading the Congregation* say, "An essential practice for being an effective leader is that one must continually examine one's own life" (Shawchuck and Heuser 1993, 36). Proverbs 4:23 says, *"Keep your heart with all vigilance, for from it flow the springs of life."* Self-examination and time spent alone with God are two things that have helped me to say, I know who I am. I must be true to who I am, despite the pressures that may come upon me to act as if I am something or someone else. I owe that to myself, and I owe it to my family. My husband and sons, who live with me every day, see me behind closed doors. They know my strengths and weaknesses. They must never see my public persona and find me to be unrecognizable to them. As much as I owe it to my church family to be a pastor of integrity, I also owe it to my husband and sons. They should see a person who is honest about who she is, outside of her robe and pulpit. They must see in me someone who can relate to their struggles because I have had my own. I offer them the hope of overcoming their struggles because of the love of God and the gift of the Holy Spirit. To this end, I have often shared with both families my past failures and weaknesses so they can see what God's transforming power can do.

Effective ministry also means being true to the God who directs my path and divinely orders my steps. The temptations to follow the popular practices that seem to draw magnanimous crowds cannot influence or persuade me to do or become someone other than what God has purposefully designed me to be.

I truly embrace the six graces as discussed in Chapter 3 that Shawchuck and Heuser believed to be vital to the life and ministry of Jesus—prayer, fasting, partaking of the Lord's Supper, the Holy Scriptures, spiritual conversation and worship (1993, 47). These graces are very important to my lifestyle. I know that God hears and answers prayers. I know that sweet communion with Christ is powerful, comforting and rewarding. I know that there is much healing in digesting the Word and partaking of the elements that represent victory on Calvary. I know that God is looking for somebody to give Him worthy praise and worship. My relationship with Jesus is sweeter as the days go by because these six graces bring my life joy.

Dr. Peter J. Gomes, author of *The Good Book,* states, "Joy is an elusive consequence of something else, and not a first cause or primary habit of mind" (1996, 232). He grew up in a joyless tradition. He remembered joyless people reading Psalm 100 (KJV), *"Make a joyful noise unto the Lord, all ye lands..."* He also remembered only singing the hymns listed in the joy section at the evening and midweek services, but never on Sunday morning. It was difficult for him to be joyful on what he called "on command." One important lesson he learned was that "joy is elusive and it cannot be summoned forth." Joy is a response (1996, 233). Gomes quotes John Habgood as saying that joy is "undeserved happiness bubbling to the surface in thanksgiving" (Gomes, 1996, 233).

Dr. Peter Gomes suggests that in order to experience joy, one should visit a black gospel church. Black people in the North and South do what all three New Testament Greek words describe as joy in song. They possess a knowledge of joy "so delicious and absolute and so paradoxical, that they have to sing" (Gomes 1996, 241). This kind of joy brings freedom and encouragement in Christ. This kind of joy makes no sense. It is without command and without a sense of duty.

Dr. Gomes quotes C. S. Lewis as saying in, *Surprised by Joy*, that joy is "an unsatisfied desire which is itself more desirable than any other satisfaction" (Gomes 1996, 242). Gomes further states that we can give ourselves pleasure, but not joy. Joy cannot be pursued and once you know joy, you will want it again. Joy reminds you of what you did not have before you gained it (1996, 242).

Gomes also says, "Joy is akin to holiness, not because of some sense of moral perfection or beauty, but because both partake of the sense of the whole, of the complete" (1996, 243). Joy is the partial becoming full, clear and complete. However, "Suffering," Gomes says, "is the context of joy even as darkness is the context for light and silence for hearing" (1996, 243–244). Once you have a joyful experience, you are restless for another.

The drug culture has tried to manufacture joy, but it has only destroyed those who were looking for shortcuts to finding it. Joy does not belong to us like property or ideas. The poem, "Eternity," written by William Blake in 1793 says:

> "He who binds to himself a joy,
> Does the winged life destroy,
> But he who kisses the joy as it flies,
> Lives in eternity's sunrise."
> (Gomes, 1996, 244)

Dr. Ken Williams and Gaylyn Williams, authors of *The Door to Joy,* state, "The more intimate we are with God, the greater our joy. This is so essential that all other keys to joy depend on it" (1999, 17). Quoting Joe Aldrich in his article, "Joy: The Illusive Fruit," they say:

> It takes time, diligence, patience and hard work to make an apple tree productive. Fruit is not instantaneous! It is a victory over weather, bugs, weeds, poor soil and neglect. If the Spirit's indwelling presence guaranteed the presence of joy, every believer would be rejoicing all the time. We're not. Joy, as a way of living, is a hard-won victory over entrenched

attitudes of apathy, pessimism, doubt, unbelief and despair (Williams and Williams 1999, 9).

God has made joy a high priority for us. The Bible mentions joy almost six hundred times. God wants our joy to be full. We can have joy no matter what happens. "Joy isn't the momentary happiness we feel when everything goes right and problems are at a minimum" (Williams and Williams 1999, 10). Joy has everything to do with our relationship with God. God gives joy, and God is our joy.

As my pastoral ministry develops, I reaffirm my being chosen and called by God. I believe that God continues to equip me for the call. I am being shaped daily through prayer, my intimate companionship with Jesus and the shepherding of my congregation. I want New Prospect Missionary Baptist Church to be a visionary church full of God's joy. We have a tremendous future before us. We can and must possess the vision that God has given us with our hearts, minds and souls. The powerful presence of the Holy Spirit has created new possibilities for our congregation. Therefore, we are keeping our eyes forward and our ears attentive to the voice of God.

If I had to identify my *golden thread,* the one thing that makes a fundamental difference in my leadership in the church, it would have four strands woven together: teaching, preaching, loving and praying. I believe that the joy ministry survey and questionnaire results indicate that I have really tried to make these four things my focus. Having the Word of God at the core of my foundation, I have interwoven these strands, and they serve as the strong underpinning of my ministry. If I stand on them, I believe I can maintain my personal integrity so that the people will listen and follow. I also believe, that having received the vision that God has for New Prospect Missionary Baptist Church, my golden thread will enable me to help the people to see it for themselves.

I am very much aware of the fact that God is using me, especially in having an impact on church growth. Great and awesome things are being accomplished, but it is God who is doing the work through me. God does the calling, and we simply follow. As a spiritual leader, I must know where I am going. I know that God has need of me. For God has need of all of His people. It takes courage to lead, meditate, pray and study the Word in order to effectively impact the lives of others. I have surrendered myself to Christ because I desire to serve with humility and much love. I know that when led by the Holy Spirit, I can do it.

I was moved by a story I read in *Leading the Congregation* (Shawchuck 1993) about a Korean sister named WhaJa Hwang. Driven by her desire to be used by God, her total surrender to Him, and her love for the poorest of God's people, she worked against all odds to minister to them, seeing that their basic needs for survival were met. Although she originally desired to use the traditional means of ministry to teach them about Jesus Christ, she learned the powerful lesson of Christ that she had to first serve them to lead them. I admired her humility, patience and determination to trust in God and to hold fast to the vision He had given her. She heard her call and obeyed. Her intimate relationship with God empowered her every step of the way. Although she was never confirmed through ordination by the denomination wherein she labored, her service to the poor, which eventually spread from Korea into other countries, confirmed in her the need to adhere to what God had spoken into her life and what He had commanded through His Word for her to do (Shawchuck 1993, 279–297). *"Truly I tell you, just as you did it to one of the least of these who are members of my family, you did it to me" (Matthew 25:40).*

Knowing that God wants to prepare us for servant leadership, I hope to motivate and inspire others to lead and serve. I would like this to be true in my ministry. I want God to guide and strengthen the leaders and the congregation. Within my church, I have to be a teacher, preacher, lover, comforter and a role model to all under my care. They have to see my heart and vision evident in what I say and do as their leader. They have to feel God's presence through how I offer spiritual and emotional support to them.

I also desire that through the Lord's guidance, we will know how to encourage and empower the members of the community that we are to serve. As a church leader, I want my ministry to bring wholeness, healing, joy and direction to this confused and dark world. I want to be a leader who pleases God. I now better understand that the church that lacks vision, purpose and leadership sets itself up for failure.

New Prospect Missionary Baptist Church is the first church I have been blessed to pastor. It has been laborious at times, but always a labor of love. I would like to think that I have been successful as the pastor and leader of New Prospect because I have been surrounded by the love of God and the support of family and members. I appreciate all the assistance from my staff, ministers, officers and family members. Over time, we have come together to see great things wrought at our hands. There is clock time, calendar time and God's time. New Prospect Missionary Baptist Church is living right now in God's time.

One of the reasons we can live and operate in God's time is because of my insistence on listening to God's voice. I am one of those women who listens to God's instructions, instead of listening to others. I am one of those women who believes that God's voice is speaking louder and clearer than any one voice. I am one of those women who heard the call and obeyed my commandment from the Lord. It is very true that this journey has not been without a struggle, but I thank God for the joys and the disappointments that have prepared me for every assignment that He has placed in my hands.

I proudly stand in line with the biblical men and women who desired to obey God; men and women like Moses, Deborah, Nehemiah, Esther and the woman at the well. As a woman leader, I proudly sit at the feet of my African-American clergywomen leaders who have stories to tell and lessons to share. I stand on the shoulders of all those strong women who answered their call to leadership. I bow in their presence. They served the Lord without titles, credentials or ordination. Here in the twenty-first century, thanks to our

God, I have all three. I am proud to link my spirit with their spirits in bringing, expanding and keeping people together for the accomplishment of common goals. I have much joy in supporting, stimulating, teaching, lifting, preaching, encouraging, praying, caring and loving my congregation. They are gifts from God. That's the way Wilma Johnson leads.

Where do I go from here? Forward, holding on to God's unchanging hand. Where do I go from here? Upward, seeking God's face and wanting more of His Presence. Where do I go from here? Onward, knowing that my feet are planted and my walk is secure. My mind is made up and I have heaven in my view. I know that the Lord is with me every step of the way. I know that my ancestors, living and deceased, every day encourage me to hang in there. I will continue to serve the Lord with gladness and thanksgiving as a woman living a life of ministry. I will not disappoint the Lord.

I often sit prayerfully, while I watch and learn as the church I pastor grows and renews itself before my eyes. New Prospect Missionary Baptist Church is taking on a whole new shape under my leadership. Things are happening that we would have never dreamed of before. The fact that our members are learning to love and trust again brings joy to my heart. The increase in membership and the obedience with their finances has been magnificent. The example that I set before them is a bright light that they can follow. As I listen to the Holy Spirit, I pray that they will not only follow me, but also emulate me. I pray that they, too, will see the benefit of submission to prayer, study and sweet communion with God. Some would lead because of the personal satisfaction of having people drawn to them. They need to be loved and so they lead for love. I seek praise and affection from my husband. I only want my congregation drawn to me because I am drawn to Christ. When they are drawn to Christ, they will be drawn to each other. Whatever I receive from my congregation, I only want it to enhance my gifts and abilities so I can better serve the Lord by loving and serving them. I am just trying to penetrate the darkness with God's light in the lives of the people I love.

I hope and pray that I can be the kind of leader that I see in the Reverend Dr. Charles G. Adams, who is my pastor. I salute him as a great navigator. He possesses all three of the qualities that John C. Maxwell said a leader must exemplify: competence, connection and character. He has influenced every area of my life.

My desire is that New Prospect Missionary Baptist Church celebrates our marriage and the spiritual closeness that makes me the leader that I am trying to be. May New Prospect ever see my commitment, zeal, determination and joy to do what the Lord says do, and may God be glorified in it all!

Afterword

Pastor Johnson's Reputation as a Joyful Pastor

Approximately five years ago, I worked as a "Theologian in the Hood" in Detroit's Summer Program for Challenged Inner City Youth. The program resulted from a collaborative effort between the state of Michigan, the city of Detroit and the churches of the city. Among the many practical questions it provoked, the most haunting theological question was: What is the relationship between the joy that we proclaim in the black church worship and the joylessness that inner city people experience daily? Numerous Detroit pastors obviously struggle with that question perennially. None has dared to engage it with more intensity and sincerity than Pastor Wilma Johnson of the New Prospect Baptist Church.

Pastor Johnson, who was mentored by the eminent Dr. Charles Adams, had made history as a recently called charismatic female pastor to New Prospect. Immediately following her call, Johnson's radically joy-laden vision of ministry was launched at this traditional black Baptist church in America's motor city. Among a circle of Detroiters, praise of Pastor Johnson's works was drowning out the negative voices of a group of black Michigan pastors' public condemnation of women in ministry. I wanted to meet the lady who I had heard led her church in giving a poor black college $40,000 in one year. I finished my work in Detroit that summer without having been blessed with meeting this great pastor face to face.

A Face-to-Face Encounter

Several years ago, I was invited to make a plenary presentation to a group of pastors and church leaders of the National Baptist Convention, USA, Inc. in Dallas, Texas. "Urban Evangelism" was the theme of the conference. Following my presentation, persons lined up to express their appreciation. During the ritual of greeting, I came face to face with Detroit's Wilma Johnson, an embodiment of Christian joy. This face-to-face encounter would be the beginning of a Christian fellowship that has grown like a tributary stream joining larger bodies of water.

Hospitable Joy in the New Prospect Church

Pastor Johnson has invited me several times to share with her church family in Detroit. Each opportunity has deepened my appreciation for her practical sense of Christian joy. During my initial visit to the New Prospect Baptist Church, I was joyfully greeted by hospitable, professional staffers. It caused an almost surreal feeling. It made me ask: What is this? Why do her staffers (paid and non-paid) display such joyful spirits? Am I hallucinating? No!

Subsequent visits have shown that the church family's joyful disposition is rooted in their leader's vision and faith that a living relationship with Jesus Christ makes for a joyful life.

The joy that I experienced during my visits to New Prospect was not in the sound of the musical instruments. It was in the sweet musical sounds of the followers of Christ joyfully doing ministry. One of my most intriguing moments of experiencing this was during a two-day conference with the men of the church. Listening to these men tell of the joy of Christ transforming their lives was a joyful sound of praise. Their testimonies defied the stereotype of black men seeing their doing ministry in the black church as a feminine thing. Instead, these men expressed their joy for having a woman pastor leading them and liberating them from their past prejudices about women ministers.

Each visit to the church leaves me joyfully proclaiming with the worshippers, "Oh, taste and see that the Lord is good!" New Prospect Baptist Church has literally made itself a joyful home to the homeless spirit as well as the homeless body, and seeks to reconcile the alienation between the two.

The Paradox of the Gift of Christian Joy

Little did I know in my initial encounter with Pastor Johnson that I would become a conversational partner with her as she prepared her manuscript for public reading. In short, my faith in God would be deepened by her story. It helped me to see with greater clarity that Christian joy is built on ultimate sacrifice. Her story helped me to see the impossibility of reveling in Pastor Johnson's charitable joy in Christ without embracing her story of a horrible, terrorized journey from childhood into young adulthood. Ironically, she kept longing for God's joy through every cycle of her troubled life. She did not abandon the church despite the terror some leader caused her in God's name. She credits God with having brought her to this point of her Christian maturation in spite of the many impediments in her path. She is profoundly convinced that God is still directing her path.

Hopefully, church leaders will read this story and struggle with our institutional challenges to liberate contemporaries from the painful relationships that terrorized the developmental life of Sister Wilma. Our silence on social justice issues is all but unbearable. The great danger of our day is that bland praise might become a substitute for genuinely worshipping God. Pastor Johnson's story of ministry ought to challenge a church's courage to do justice, love mercy and walk upright with God.

Pastor Johnson's story is a gift of joy to a public that suffers from the sorrow of walking in darkness and being cut off from the marvelous light of salvation. The lack of organic relationship with Christ and each other is referenced in John's gospel. Johnson's story of ministry reflects the fact that she has found that *joy* that only the vine and the vine grower can give. Jesus speaks of Himself as being the vine and His disciples being the branches. Jesus also speaks of His Father as being the vine grower who has the right to prune fruitless branches in Him.

Obedience to God and Christ is the prerequisite for receiving joy. It makes the relationship organic in nature. Jesus' word, according to John's gospel, makes this fact rather transparent:

> *If you abide in me, and my words abide in you, ask for whatever you wish, and it will be done for you. My Father is glorified by this, that you bear much fruit and become my disciples. As the Father has loved me, so I have loved you; abide in my love. If you keep my commandments, you will abide in my love, just as I have kept my Father's commandments and abide in his love. I have said these things to you so that my joy may be in you, and that your joy may be complete (John 15:7–11).*

This clearly indicates that the gift of Christ's joy is based on an organic relationship with Jesus Christ and God. John's gospel places these words by Jesus near the time that He is preparing for His trial and crucifixion. Paradoxically, Jesus' promise of the gift of joy comes in the shadow of this tragic moment in His life. In His priestly prayer to His Father, Jesus expresses a desire for His joy to be complete in His disciples before his death ascension: *"But now I am coming to you, and I speak these things in the world so that they may have my joy made complete in themselves" (John 17:13).*

When Pastor Johnson speaks of giving away her joy, she is dealing with the great paradox of Christian gift giving. Christ gifts us so that giving and receiving are inseparable. In using the Psalmist Model of Spiritual Joy, Johnson is giving away both what is hers and not hers. Christ reminds us that it is His joy that has been given to us. If we are to grow in this joyful relationship with Christ, we must give away the joy He has given us. This is why the joy of Jesus' resurrection cannot be separated from His crucifixion.

Riggins R. Earl, Jr., Ph.D.
Professor, Ethics and Theology
The Interdenominational Theological Center
Atlanta, Georgia

Appendix

Appendix A

Church Covenant

Having been led, as we believe, by the Spirit of God, to receive the Lord Jesus Christ as our Savior, and on the profession of our faith, having been baptized in the name of the Father, the Son and the Holy Ghost, we do now, in the presence of God, angels and this assembly, most solemnly and joyfully enter into covenant with one another, as one body in Christ.

We promise by the aid of the Holy Spirit to forsake the paths of sin, and to walk in the ways of holiness all the days of our lives. With this view, we engage to strive together for the advancement of this church in knowledge, holiness and comfort; to promote its prosperity and spirituality; to sustain its worship, ordinances, discipline and doctrines; to contribute cheerfully by tithing, as taught in the Bible, for the support of the ministry, the expenses of the church, the relief of the poor and the spread of the gospel throughout all nations.

We also engage to maintain family and secret devotion to religiously educate our children; to seek the salvation of our kindred and acquaintances; to walk circumspectly in the world; to be just in our dealings, faithful in our engagements, and exemplary in our deportment; to avoid all tattling, back-biting, and excessive anger; to oppose all unloving acts and attitudes in all walks of (life) toward any of God's children;

and to be zealous in our efforts to advance the kingdom of our Savior.

We further agree to walk together in Christian love and watchfulness, giving and receiving admonition with meekness and affection; to remember each other in prayer, to aid each other in sickness and distress, to cultivate Christian sympathy in feeling and courtesy in speech; to be slow to take offense, but always ready for reconciliation, and being mindful of the rules of our Savior, to secure it without delay.

We moreover engage that when we remove from this place, we will as soon as possible unite with some other church where we can carry out the spirit of this covenant and the principles of God's Word. Humbly confessing our past sins, we pray for grace and strength to keep these, our holy vows, for the sake of Jesus Christ, our Lord. AMEN!

Appendix B

List of Donations

Below is a partial list of recipients of donations and gifts from New Prospect Missionary Baptist Church.

American Baptist College

Home Mission Board (National Baptist Convention, USA, Inc.)

NAACP

Charles H. Wright African American Museum

Michigan District Baptist Association

Oakland Social Services

Junior Diabetes Research Foundation

Another Chance Ministry

Sinai-Grace Hospital

The Leukemia and Lymphoma Society

International Women's Conference (IWC)

Girlfriends

Wayne County Community College

Campus Crusade for Christ

First Institutional Baptist Church, Phoenix, Arizona (Mission Ministry)

Race for the Cure

Mumford High School

Simon House

Mariner's Inn

Pasteur Elementary School

AIDS Walk Detroit

Boy Scouts of America

American Baptist Churches of Michigan

International Women's Consortium

My Sister's Place

Word Restorations Ministries

Friendship House (Harvest Food Ministry)

St. Gerard Catholic Community (Haiti Mission)

Westside Christian Academy

United Negro College Fund

Habitat for Humanity

National Baptist Convention, USA, Inc.

Appendix C

Pastor's Holiday Greeting

Greetings and blessings my church family!
Holy Advent, Merry Christmas and Happy New Year to you!

The season of Advent and Christmas is a season of hope. The very meaning of this season is about someone coming. Jesus Christ is coming!

During this joyous season, the church proclaims the righteousness of God, which is real hope. We cannot live without hope. Anticipating what God is going to do should energize us for faithful living.

This is the season to prepare ourselves for the visit of God's salvation. God brings newness in the birth of Christ. God is doing a new thing among the people of God.

A brand new year of praise is coming. Let us lift up our heads, and let our hearts be strengthened. Let us tell the world that all is not lost. We do have a hope that is eternal and true. Let us grow in the love of God and share that love with others.

May the Christ Child, who is Lord of Lords, bless your home and family each day of this season. May Jesus live and reign with you in the unity of the Holy Spirit—one God, now and forever.

Let us rejoice! Let us worship! Let us love!

With much love and joy from the first family,

Deacon Dave, Pastor J, Davey and Brian Johnson

Appendix D

Holiday Service Calendar

First Sunday of Advent
" Jesus: Song of Hope"

November 30, 2003
Luke 1:67–79

Second Sunday of Advent
"Jesus: Song of Peace"

December 7, 2003
Luke 2:22–39

Third Sunday of Advent
"Jesus: Song of Joy"

December 14, 2003
Luke 1:46–55

Fourth Sunday of Advent
"Jesus: Song of Love"

December 21, 2003
Luke 2:1–20

**Christmas Gathering/Pastor's Birthday
Celebration
December 21, 2003 @ 5:00 p.m.
Play and Reception**

Christmas Eve
Musical Cantata / Worship Service
"A Child Is Born"

December 24, 2003
6:00 p.m.
Isaiah 9:6

First Sunday After Christmas
**"Why Would Anyone Want to Kill
Baby Jesus?"**

December 28, 2003
Matthew 2:13–23

Watch Night Worship
"Facing Fear of the Future"

December 31, 2003
10:00 p.m.
Jeremiah 29:11–13

First Sunday of 2004
"Depending on God"

January 4, 2004
Psalm 91

Appendix E

Ministry Joy Survey

Survey Topic: How does this pastor's psalmist pastoral/ministry style called "Giving Away My Joy" attract people?

1. Gender: M   F

2. Age: 12–26   27–41   42–56   57–71   72+

3. Are you a member of New Prospect Missionary Baptist Church?

   Yes   No   If yes, what year did you join?

4. If you are a visitor, how did you hear about New Prospect Missionary Baptist Church?
   Newspaper   Radio   Family/Friends
   Yellow Pages   Other

5. How many Sundays out of the month do you attend the Sunday Worship Services at New Prospect Missionary Baptist Church?

   1–2   3–5

6. Select the **three** most important areas that keep you attending this place of worship?

   Fellowship   Preaching / Teaching

   Music   Outreach   Youth Programs   Other

7. Are your spiritual needs being met here at New Prospect Missionary Baptist Church?

   Yes   If yes, how?   No   If no, why?

8. What do you need most **from** a pastor and **in** a pastor?

   Please select the most important **five.**

Compassion	Prayer Life
Word of God	Preaching/Teaching Skills
Honesty	Comfort
Leadership Ability	Integrity
Friendly	Commitment
Encouragement	Godly Lifestyle
Sensitivity	Sincerity
Spirit-filled	Other

9. Does this psalmist pastoral/ministry style of "Giving Away My Joy" help you give away your joy?

   Yes   No   Please explain.

10. Through this fellowship and the way I do ministry here, how has God provided your life with joy?

11. How does my joy that I give away through music and praise lift your spirits?

12. What sermon preached by this "joyful pastor" has given you the most joy?

Appendix F

Gender and Age of Survey Group

Age Categories	Females	%	Males	%
12–26	53	7	24	3
27–41	125	17	40	5
42–56	216	29	55	7
56–71	135	18	39	5
72+	41	5	21	3
Totals	570	76	179	23

Total Surveyed   749

NOTES:
- On the day the survey was conducted, a little over three-quarters of the congregation were females.
- Nearly fifty percent, or half of those who participated were women between the ages of 42 and 71.
- It is interesting to note that all categories of men were fairly and equally distributed, although more of the men were between the ages of 27 and 71.

Appendix G

Monthly Worship Attendance

Respondents were asked to report whether they attended worship services 1–2 or 3–5 Sundays per month.

Attendance 3–5 Sundays Per Month

Age Categories	Females	%	Males	%
12–26	53	80	24	50
27–41	125	72	40	87
42–56	216	84	55	70
56–71	135	86	39	89
72+	41	80	21	80
Totals	570	76	179	23

Total Surveyed   749

NOTES:
As this table indicates, generally eighty percent of the respondents attend church on a regular basis, 3–5 times per month. The only group that was markedly irregular in its attendance was the young group of males who attended only fifty percent of the worship services.

Appendix H

Reasons for Attending

Respondents were asked to select the three most important areas that encouraged them to attend church.

Reason	Females	%	Males	%
Fellowship	441	77	139	78
Preaching	539	95	151	84
Music	308	54	95	53
Outreach	120	21	35	20
Youth	18	0.3	11	0.6
Totals	570		179	

NOTES:

As the data suggests, the most important reason respondents attended worship service was for the preaching/teaching. Ninety-five percent of the female respondents and eighty-four percent of the male respondents came to church to hear the preaching. It is interesting to note that more male respondents were attracted to the church for fellowship.

AppendixI

Most Important Pastor Characteristics

Respondents were asked to select five out of sixteen things needed most from and in a pastor. The following responses were received from 570 females and 179 males.

Characteristic	Females	%
Word of God	431	75.7
Preaching Skills	423	74.3
Compassion	246	43.2
Honesty	237	41.6
Leadership	227	39.9
Total Surveyed	570	
	Males	**%**
Word of God	127	71
Preaching Skills	125	69.9
Honesty	82	45.8
Prayer Life	73	40.8
Leadership	59	33
Total Surveyed	179	

NOTES:
It is interesting to note that while the female respondents chose compassion as a primary need, the male respondents selected prayer life instead. The other top four needs were the same for both groups.

Appendix J

Ministry Joy Questionnaire

Name_____ Male or Female ____

Age: 18–35   36–50   50 or above
Please circle one.

What year did you join New Prospect Missionary Baptist Church? _____

1. What do you think the leadership of a pastor involves?

2. Give your reasons for church growth at New Prospect Missionary Baptist Church.

3. Give me your theological definition of joy.

4. Based on your definition, describe the level of joy here at New Prospect Missionary Baptist Church.

5. Has the theme of "theological joy," demonstrated by this pastor, impacted your ministry as a Christian?
   If yes, how?   If no, please explain.

6. Do you have a new or different theological perspective towards ministry, pastors or the church?

7. Has the preaching and Bible teaching encouraged or had any impact on how you practice ministry with others? If so, in what ways?

8. Has the preaching and Bible teaching had an impact on your relationship with God? If so, in what ways?

9. We have a Biblical mandate for stewardship. Has your understanding of stewardship changed?
   If so, in what ways?

10. In what way, if any, have you personally been changed by my pastoral leadership style?

11. If applicable, please describe New Prospect Missionary Baptist Church before I became the pastor?

12. Please describe New Prospect Missionary Baptist Church today?

Bibliography

Anderson, Robert C. *The Effective Pastor.* Chicago: Moody Press, 1985.

Baker, Benjamin Stanley. *The Battle Is the Lord's.* Southfield, MI: Pastor Baker Ministry, 2002.

Brueggemann, Walter. *The Message of the Psalms.* Minneapolis, MN: Augsbury Publishing House, 1984.

Cavanagh, Michael E. *The Effective Minister.* San Francisco: Harper & Row Publishers, 1986.

Dale, Robert D. *Leadership for a Changing Church.* Nashville: Abingdon Press, 1998.

Davis, Sam. *When the Multitude Comes.* North Augusta, SC: Joyful Sound Ministry, Inc., 2001.

Dever, Mark. *Nine Marks of a Healthy Church.* Wheaton, IL: Crossway Books, 2000.

Gomes, Peter, Jr. *The Good Book.* New York: William Morrow and Company, Inc., 1996.

Harris, Forrest E., Sr. *Ministry for Social Crisis.* Macon, GA: Mercer University Press, 1993.

Longenecker, Harold L. *Growing Leaders by Design.* Grand Rapids, MI: Kregel Resources, 1995.

Malphurs, Aubrey. *The Dynamics of Church Leadership.* Grand Rapids, MI: Baker Book House, 1999.

Maxwell, John C. *The 21 Irrefutable Laws of Leadership.* Nashville: Thomas Nelson, Inc., 1998.

Nelson, William R. *Ministry Formation for Effective Leadership.* Nashville: Abingdon Press, 1988.

Rainer, Thom S. *Surprising Insights From the Unchurched.* Grand Rapids, MI: Zondervan, 2001.

Russell, Bob. *When God Builds a Church.* West Monroe, LA: Howard Publishing Company Inc., 2000.

Shawchuck, Norman and Roger Heuser. *Leading the Congregation.* Nashville: Abingdon Press, 1993.

Stewart, Carlyle Fielding, III. *African American Church Growth.* Nashville: Abingdon Press, 1994.

Wagner, E. Glenn. *Escape From Church, Inc.* Grand Rapids, MI: Zondervan, 1999.

Wheatley, Margaret. *Leadership and the New Science.* San Francisco: Berrett-Koehler Publishers, 1999.

Wilkes, Gene C. *Jesus on Leadership.* Wheaton, IL: Tyndale House Publishers, 1998.

Williams, Ken L. and Gaylyn R. Williams. *The Door to Joy.* Colorado Springs, CO: Relationship Resources, Inc., 1999.

About the Author

The Reverend Dr. Wilma Robena Johnson is an ordained Baptist minister and woman of God. On March 1, 1999, she became the senior pastor of New Prospect Missionary Baptist Church in Detroit, Michigan. Her ministry journey began in September of 1974. She was licensed by Rev. Russell Fox, Sr., pastor of Mt. Olive Baptist Church in East Orange, New Jersey and the late Dr. E. A. Freeman at First Baptist Church in Kansas City, Kansas. In 1992, she was ordained by Rev. Dr. Charles Gilchrist Adams for full-time ministry. She joyfully served at Hartford Memorial Baptist Church as Assistant to the Pastor in Christian Nurture for almost nine years.

She has a bachelor's degree in business administration, a master's degree in pastoral ministry and a doctorate in ministry. Her article about "Priscilla" appears in the *New Women of Color Study Bible* (Nia Publishing, 2001).

Dr. Johnson has received numerous awards and commendations. She is the first female senior pastor to become a member of and preach at the Council of Baptist Pastors of Detroit and Vicinity, Inc. She is the third vice president of the Detroit Chapter–NAACP. She is a member of the Board of Trustees for the American Baptist College in Nashville, Tennessee. She is also a trustee of the Home Mission Board of the National Baptist Convention, USA, Inc. In 2002, she received the Pastor of the Year Award from the Southeast Michigan District Chapter of the Southern Christian Leadership Conference (SCLC).

Dr. Johnson is in demand as a public speaker. Over the years, she has preached the gospel of Jesus Christ and conducted workshops. Her speaking engagements, revivals, retreats, conferences and seminars have taken her throughout the United States. She gladly lets everyone know that she is born again! Her motto is "Jesus is the best thing that ever happened to me."

Dr. Johnson and her husband, Deacon David L. Johnson, have two sons, David Lawrence and Brian Langston.